Interactive
book with
**TIPCODES**

Tipbook

# Keyboard
## and Digital Piano

e Complete Guide

" The Tipbook Series is a
splendid addition to
the music field. "
— Pianoeducation.org

" This guide
has successfully
achieved the difficult
task of being relevant for
both beginners and
experts. "
—Music Educators Journal

Roland

The Complete Guide
to Your Instrument!

GOER

Includes Chord
Charts!

# Tipbook
# Keyboard
## *The Complete Guide* and Digital Piano

Hugo Pinksterboer

# Tipbook
# Keyboard
## and Digital Piano

*The Complete Guide*

**HAL•LEONARD®**

## *The Complete Guide to Your Instrument!*

The publisher and author have done their best to ensure the accuracy and timeliness of all the information in this Tipbook; however, they can accept ............y for any loss, injury, or inconvenience sustained as a result ......... or advice contained in this book. Trademarks, user names, and certain illustrations have been used in this book solely to identify the products or instruments discussed. Such use does not imply endorsement by or affiliation with the trademark owner(s).

First edition published in 2004 by
The Tipbook Company bv, The Netherlands

Second edition published in 2009 by
Hal Leonard Books
An Imprint of Hal Leonard Corporation
7777 West Bluemound Road
Milwaukee, WI 53213

Trade Book Division Editorial Offices
19 West 21st Street, New York, NY 10010

Printed in the United States of America

Book design by Gijs Bierenbroodspot

Library of Congress Cataloging-in-Publication Data

Pinksterboer, Hugo.
  Tipbook keyboard and digital piano : the complete guide /
  Hugo Pinksterboer.
  — 2nd ed.
      p. cm.
  Includes bibliographical references and index.
  ISBN 978-1-4234-4277-6
  1. Electronic piano. 2. Keyboard instruments.  I. Title.
  ML697.P56 2009
  786.5'919—dc22

                              2008047166


www.halleonard.com

## Thanks!

For their information, their expertise, their time, and their help we'd like to thank the following keyboard and digital piano experts:

Robert Schmidt, Leon Padmos (M-Works), Nathan Cairo, Kim Burton, Dick Barten, Eddy Dieters and Joost van Leeuwen, Allard Krijger and Eppo Schaap (*Interface*), Luc Wäckerlin, Aard van Asseldonk (Generalmusic), René de Graaff, Rick Oldersom and Michel Lamine, André Rietveld (Yamaha Music), Christian Scheck and Kristof Mertens (Roland Benelux), Carin Tielen, Bram de Jong, Auke van der Gaast, and Matthieu Vermeulen.

Special thanks go to Fran Schreuder for his contributions to the chord chart section, and to Charli Green for his assistance.

## About the Author

Journalist, writer, and musician **Hugo Pinksterboer**, author of The Tipbook Series, has published hundreds of interviews, articles, and reviews for national and international music magazines.

## About the Designer

Illustrator, designer, and musician **Gijs Bierenbroodspot** has worked as an art director for a wide variety of magazines and has developed numerous ad campaigns. While searching in vain for information about saxophone mouthpieces, he got the idea for this series of books on music and musical instruments. He is responsible of the layout and illustrations for all of the Tipbooks.

## Acknowledgments

Cover photo: René Vervloet and Gijs Bierenbroodspot
Editors: Robert L. Doerschuk and Meg Clark
Proofreaders: Nancy Bishop

## Anything missing?

Any omissions? Any areas that could be improved? Please go to www.tipbook.com to contact us, or send an email to info@tipbook.com. Thanks!

# Contents

# *Introduction*

*Are you thinking about buying a keyboard or a digital piano, or do you want to learn more about the instrument you already have? If so, this book will tell you everything you need to know: the main features and characteristics of these instruments, auditioning, testing keyboards and digital pianos, and judging their sound, MIDI and other connections; maintenance, the history and the family of the piano and the keyboard — and much more.*

Having read this Tipbook, you'll be able to get the most out of your instrument, to buy the best keyboard or piano you can, and to easily grasp any other literature on the subject, from books and magazines to online publications.

### The first four chapters
If you have just started playing, or haven't yet begun, pay particular attention to the first four chapters. They explain the basics of the instruments and their endless possibilities, and tell you about learning to play, and about buying or renting an instrument. The information provided in these chapters also fully prepares you to read the rest of the book.

### Core chapters
Chapter 5 deals with the main features of keyboards and digital pianos, ranging from the various types of keys and keyboards to their pedals, sequencers and arpeggiators, effects and controllers,

displays, layers and splits, and so on. Chapter 6 is dedicated to judging instruments on its sound, including information on their built-in sound systems. The next chapter tells you more about the features of automatic accompaniment systems, while Chapter 8 takes you a short tour along the various connectors that you may find on these instruments. Chapter 9 introduces you to the world of MIDI. Digital instrument require little maintenance, but there are plenty of tips that will help you enjoy your instrument for many years. They're covered in Chapter 10.

### Background information

Chapters 11 to 13 offer useful background information, shedding light on the history and the family members of the digital piano and the keyboard, and introducing you to the companies that make these fascinating instruments.

### Street prices

Please note that all price indications listed on the following pages are based on estimated street prices in US dollars.

### Glossary

The glossary at the end of the book briefly explains most of the terms you'll come across as a keyboard player. Also included are a complete index of terms, and a couple of pages for essential notes on your equipment.

### Chord charts

As an essential extra, this Tipbook offers a comprehensive section on chords, including basic theory on chords, chord symbols, inversions, and helpful tips as well as hundreds of chord charts – so you can start playing right away. Enjoy!

*— Hugo Pinksterboer*

# See and Hear What You Read with Tipcodes

## *www.tipbook.com*

*In addition to the many illustrations on the following pages, Tipbooks offer you a new way to see — and even hear — what you are reading about.*
*The Tipcodes that you will come across throughout this book provide instant access to short videos, sound files, and other additional information at www.tipbook.com.*

Here's how it works. Below the paragraph on synthesizer and pad sounds on page 95 is a short section marked **Tipcode KEYS-016**. Type in that code on the Tipcode page at www.tipbook.com and you will hear a brief demonstration of these sounds. Similar sound files are available on a variety of subjects; other Tipcodes link to a short video.

**TIPCODE**

**Tipcode KEYS-016**
*Typical pad and synthesizer sounds can be found on any home keyboard. Here are two examples.*

### Repeat

If you miss something the first time, you can of course replay the Tipcode. And if it all happens too fast, use the pause button beneath the movie window.

### Tipcodes listed

For your convenience, the Tipcodes presented in this book are listed on page 172. The keyboard Tipcodes include demonstrations of various types of effects, electric piano sounds, fine tuning, filters, envelope generators, and more, adding an extra dimension to this book.

First, make your selection: Tipcode, chords and fingering charts, or the glossary.

The Tipcode window displays videos, fingering charts, chords, or a glossary of the terms used in this book.

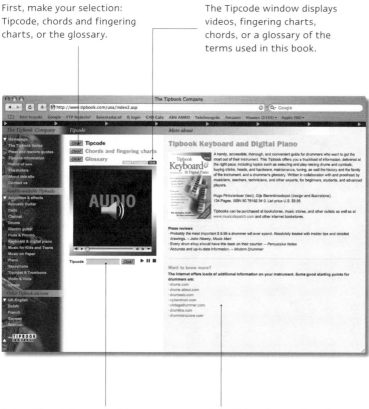

Enter a Tipcode here and click on the button. Want to see it again? Click again.

These links take you directly to other interesting sites.

### Plug-ins

If the software you need to view the videos is not yet installed on your computer, you'll automatically be told which software you need, and where you can download it. This type of software is free. Questions? Check out 'About this site' at www.tipbook.com.

### Still more at www.tipbook.com

You can find even more information at www.tipbook.com. For instance, you can look up words in the glossaries of *all* the Tipbooks published to date. There are chord diagrams for guitarists and pianists; fingering charts for saxophonists, clarinetists, and flutists; and rudiments for drummers. Also included are links to most of the websites mentioned in the *Want to Know More?* section of each Tipbook.

# Tipbook
# Keyboard
## and Digital Piano
*The Complete Guide*

# 1

# A Keyboard Player?

As a keyboard player, you learn to master one of the
most versatile instruments around — whether it is a
digital piano, or a home keyboard. You can play almost
any style of music. You can play the instrument solo or
in a band, you can hook up it up to other instruments,
or connect it to a computer and use the computer as a
recording studio or an interactive
tutor, and so on. What more do you want?

This chapter mainly looks at what you can do with a keyboard or a digital piano. If you're not sure which instrument of the two you should get, this should help you make that decision.

### Pianist

If you would like to play the piano, you may prefer a *digital piano* to a traditional *acoustic piano*. Why? A digital piano allows you to practice without bothering your neighbors or housemates, it doesn't need to be tuned, it hardly needs maintenance, and it's usually much less expensive.

*Digital pianos usually offer fewer sounds and features than keyboards.*

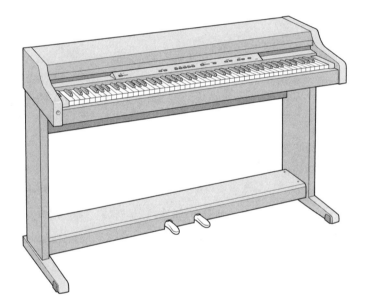

### Keyboardist

If you'd like to have easy access to the sounds of hundreds of different instruments, from organs to guitars and from flutes to saxophones; and if you want to be able to sound like a full band all by yourself, you're better off with a *keyboard*, also known as a *portable keyboard* or *home keyboard*.

### Solo

Both pianos and keyboards are great solo instruments: You can play all by yourself in a wide variety of styles. That said, keyboards

**2**

are less often used in jazz and classical music; pianos are much better suited for those styles.

## Automatic band

If you want to play solo, a keyboard can provide you with a complete automatic band with a bassist, a drummer, strings, horns, a guitarist or a pianist, and other virtual instrumentalists. The band or the orchestra follows you as you play. With a keyboard, you are a one-man band in the true sense of the word.

## Practice partner

This *automatic accompaniment* feature of the instrument also turns into a great practice partner: You can rehearse your parts at home while the instrument replaces your band.

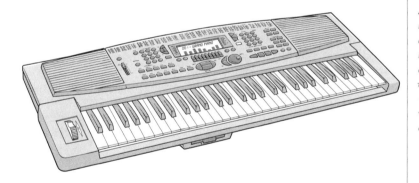

A keyboard has numerous sounds and a built-in band — the automatic accompaniment — that can play various styles of music.

## In a band

You can use a keyboard in a band too. Just switch off the automatic accompaniment and use the instrument to play a piano part, string harmonies, flute melodies, a guitar solo, or whatever else you like.

## Synthesizer

However, if you play in a band, a *synthesizer* may be more suitable. Synthesizers don't have automatic accompaniment (you don't need that in a band), but they allow you to create, edit and play a wider variety of sounds than most keyboards do. There's more on synthesizers in Chapter 12.

3

> ### Any style
> From jazz to techno, from country to Latin, from classical to ethnic music, up-to-date keyboards provide you with accompaniments in the latest musical styles, and many instruments can simply be updated online.

### New songs

If you want to write your own music on a home keyboard or digital piano, you can use its built-in recorder to play a new song to your band members, giving them an idea of what it should sound like. Or you can connect your instrument to your computer and have it print your composition, for example.

### More

There are many more things that make pianos and keyboard very attractive instruments. Some examples:

- On keyboards and pianos, every note has **its own key**. This makes these instruments very accessible for new players. You want a higher note? Move to the right. Want a lower one? Move to the left. That's about as easy as it can be.

- Learning to play a keyboard instrument really well takes just as long as learning any other instrument. But it **won't take you that long** to play something that sounds acceptable, or even impressive: You play a simple melody, and the keyboard provides you with a full band.

- A growing number of instruments features **an onboard tutor** that helps you learn to play the instrument more easily.

- Keyboards start at **very friendly prices**, and a professional quality digital piano costs about as much a low budget acoustic piano.

- Most electronic keyboard instruments have **built-in amplification**, so there's no need to buy separate speakers and amps — unless you're ready for a public performance.

4

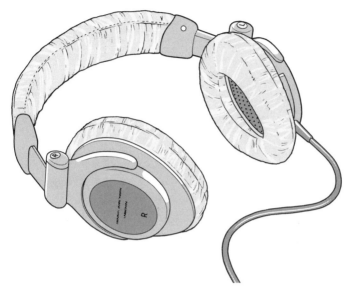

*You can play these instruments at any time, day or night.*

### Keyboard?

The word 'keyboard' is a bit confusing. Originally, it indicated the range of black and white keys that you find on pianos, organs, and synthesizers. These are all *keyboard instruments*. Someone who plays 'keys' plays a keyboard instrument.

### Keyboard!

Later on, 'keyboard' grew to be short for home keyboard or portable keyboard, two terms that are used interchangeably. It adds to the confusion that the term 'keyboard' is also used for synthesizers and all other keyboard instruments.

### Multiple instruments

Mastering one keyboard instrument gives you easy access to most other keyboard instruments: After all, the layout of the keys is the same on each one. Though different keyboard instruments require very different playing techniques, there are many keyboard players who play them all. After all, it's not that unusual to see a band with someone who uses a digital piano, a synthesizer, and even more keyboard instruments in one setup!

5

# 2

# A Quick Tour

*Home keyboards often look quite intimidating, with dozens of buttons, knobs, sliders, and other controls. Most digital pianos are easier on the eye. Here's a quick tour to take the mystery out of both. Chapters 5 to 9 deal with these subjects in greater detail.*

First, the keys that make up the keyboard or *manual*. If you take a closer look, you will see that these keys are divided into alternate groups of two and three black keys. This grouping makes it easy to find the notes you want to play.

**Tipcode KEYS-001**
Tipcode KEYS-001 shows you were the C and F keys on a keyboard are, and plays an octave.

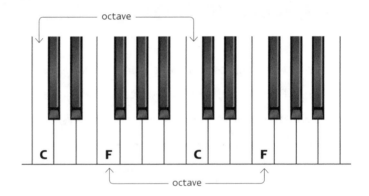

### The C and the F
Two examples:

- The white key to the left of each group of **two** black keys is a C.

- The white key to the left of each group of **three** black keys is an F.

### Octave
There are always eight white keys from one C to the next. Such a group of eight is called an *octave*. Within each octave you will find five black keys.

8

### Seven octaves

Acoustic pianos and most digital pianos have 88 keys. This adds up to a little more than seven octaves. With these 88 keys you can player lower notes than a bass guitar, and higher notes than a piccolo, the very smallest flute.

### Fewer keys

Most home keyboards or portable keyboards have fewer keys. If you're serious about playing, then go for one with at least 61 keys (i.e., five octaves).

### Samples

When you play the keys of a keyboard or a digital piano, you are actually playing back digital recordings. These recordings, *samples*, are stored in the instrument's memory. There are series of samples for every type of sound: one series for the grand piano sound, one for the rock organ sound, and so on.

### Loud and soft

Most keyboards and all pianos have *touch sensitive* keyboards: The harder you play the keys, the louder the sound will be. The instrument's overall volume is set with a *volume control.*

# DIGITAL PIANOS

Digital pianos are often used instead of an acoustic piano. When you play the keys of an acoustic piano, you make a series of felt hammers hit the pianos strings. This gives the keys a certain feel. Good digital pianos mimic this feel, usually by incorporating small hammers in the instrument's mechanism or *action.*

### Other instruments

To make a digital piano sound like an acoustic one, it houses digital recordings of all the notes of one or more acoustic pianos. Samples of a grand piano are usually included as well. Most digital pianos can also play back the sounds of other instruments. Next

9

to various types of acoustic pianos (regular piano, rock piano, honky-tonk, etc.), you may have a choice of electric pianos, one or more organ sounds, and a harpsichord, for example. A number of non-keyboard sounds may be included too, such as a choir or strings (e.g., violins).

**TIPCODE**

**Tipcode KEYS-002**
This Tipcode offers a sample of various sounds featured in a digital piano.

### Different types

There are various basic types of digital pianos.

- A **traditional digital piano** often looks like a small-sized acoustic piano, either with or without a full cabinet below the actual keyboard. It typically features a limited number of piano and piano-related sounds.

A stage piano.

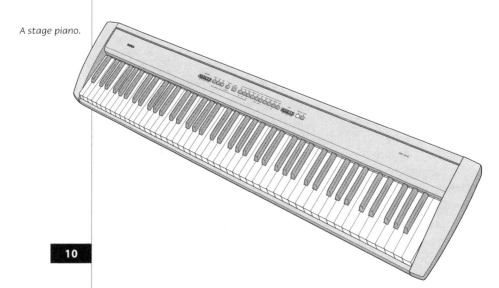

- An **interactive digital piano** looks about the same, but it shares a number of features with home keyboards, ranging from an automatic accompaniment to hundreds of sounds, a hard disk, or an onboard tutor.

- Both types of instruments are available in **grand piano** design as well.

- **Stage pianos** are built for onstage use, typically featuring a solid build quality construction and a few dozen easily accessible sounds. Some stage piano have small built-in speakers, for practicing purposes only.

# HOME KEYBOARDS

In effect, a home keyboard is a band-in-a-box, with an onboard drummer, a bass player, a string section (e.g., violinists) and a host of other electronic 'musicians' that are waiting to join in. Just press the start button, hit a key with your left hand, and the orchestra starts playing in the style you have selected: rock, waltz, jazz, hardcore, country, techno, dance — you name it.

### Sounds
Home keyboards or portable keyboards usually have anywhere from a hundred to more than a thousand sounds, tones or voices to choose from: organs, electric and acoustic guitars, basses, violins, cellos, saxophones, flutes, trombones, basses, drums, cowbells, vocals, ethnic instruments, synthesizer sounds, effects (applause, helicopters, etc.), and much more.

### Keyboard or piano?
Each keyboard features a number of piano sounds as well. So why bother buying a digital piano? Because its action is closer to that of an acoustic piano, because it has the required number of keys (usually 88), and because most digital pianos sound more like their acoustic relatives.

11

### The keyboard

The home keyboard is a descendant of the organ, and its keys usually feel like organ keys. They requires less finger strength than piano-type keys do, so they're easier to play. But if you want to learn to play the piano, you're much better off with a digital piano featuring a piano-like hammer action.

### Hammer action home keyboard

*Some 'piano focused' home keyboards are perfectly suited for piano playing, featuring an 88-key hammer action keyboard. Alternatively, you can get a digital piano with keyboard features (see below), or even a hybrid piano (see page 159).*

### Chords

The only way to play chords (three or more notes at a time) on a piano is to actually hit all the right notes. On keyboards, you can play chords using just one or two fingers: Keyboards have a chord recognition system.

### Automatic accompaniment

The automatic accompaniment section of a keyboard is like a virtual band. Once you press the *start* button, the band will follow the chords you play. The only thing you have to do first is tell the band whether it should play jazz, rock, Latin, or any other style, and which instruments to use.

**TIPCODE**

AUDIO

**Tipcode KEYS-003**
Play this Tipcode for a brief demonstration of intros and endings.

12

## Intros and endings

Many songs start with an intro. Press the *intro* button, and the instrument will play a musical introduction that perfectly fits the style of music you have selected. Likewise, keyboards feature one or more *endings* for the available styles.

## Variations and fills

A button marked *variation* produces a slightly different accompaniment pattern, which you can use in the chorus of a song, for example; for the next verse, you may go back to the *main* or *basic pattern*. The *fill* or *fill-in* button produces a very brief variation, usually featuring a drum roll of some sort. Fills are often used to mark the beginning of the next section of a song.

**Tipcode KEYS-004**
This Tipcode demonstrates what variations and fills can sound like.

TIPCODE

## Pianos with auto accompaniments

As mentioned before, some digital pianos also have built-in accompaniments. Depending on the brand, these instruments are known as *interactive pianos, ensemble pianos, rhythm pianos, intelligent pianos,* or *digital ensembles,* among other names.

Accompaniment controls: start, stop, fill-in, variation...

13

# COMMON FEATURES

Now that you know the main differences between keyboards and digital pianos, it's time to take a look at some of their common features. The illustrations on these pages show where everything is located on a typical instrument. Contrary to what you may think, the basic design of these instruments hasn't changed that much over the years.

*Keyboard (Yamaha).*

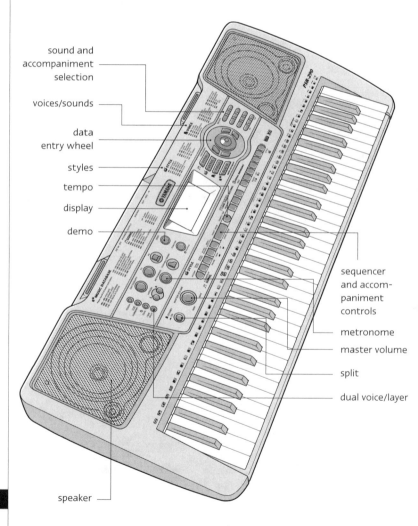

sound and accompaniment selection

voices/sounds

data entry wheel

styles

tempo

display

demo

sequencer and accompaniment controls

metronome

master volume

split

dual voice/layer

speaker

**14**

on/off    transpose    split    metronome    reverb (effect)    recorder (sequencer)

*Digital piano.*

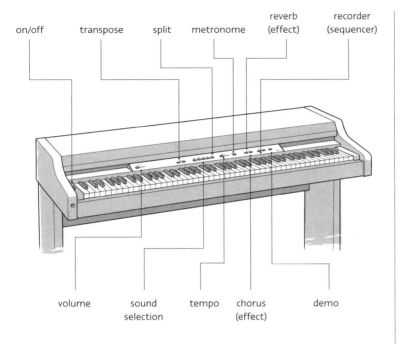

volume    sound selection    tempo    chorus (effect)    demo

**TIP**

### Demo

*Most keyboards and digital pianos have a demo button. Hit it to listen what the instrument is capable of. Some instruments have a hundred or more demo songs on board. These can also be used to entertain the audience while you're having an intermission!*

### Speakers

On keyboards, the *speakers* are often in full view, sitting behind a *speaker grille*. On pianos they're usually hidden. Amplification on both instruments is taken care of by an onboard amplifier. Pianos typically have larger speakers and more powerful amps, contributing to the quality of their sound.

### Display

Most keyboards have a *display* that shows a lot of information, ranging from the sounds and music style you have selected to the

15

notes and the chords you play, the tempo, the bar you are in, and more. Most pianos have fairly basic displays that simply show the currently selected sound. Other *parameters* are shown as you change them (volume, tuning, etc.).

### Selecting sounds and styles

Pianos with a limited number of sounds usually have a direct button for each sound. Simply press the button with the sound you're looking for, and start playing. Instruments that feature a larger variety of voices have no room for dedicated buttons. You select sounds with either a numeric keypad, by using a combination of keys, or by making a selection from the instrument's touch screen, for example.

*Selecting sounds on a basic digital piano.*

### Tempo

When you choose a style on a keyboard, the instrument usually selects an appropriate tempo for that style. Tempo buttons allow you to make the band play faster or slower.

### Metronome

Most digital pianos have a built-in *metronome*: a device that marks the tempo with a steady series of clicks or beeps. The tempo is set in a number of beats per minute (BPM), typically between 40 or less to 250 or up. Most metronomes allow you to select a specific time signature (e.g., $\frac{3}{4}, \frac{4}{4}, \frac{6}{8}$), marked by different sound or an accent at the first beat of each bar. Some can play odd time signatures too (e.g., $\frac{5}{4}$ or $\frac{9}{8}$).

*Metronome controls (left)*

## Pads

Keyboards often have a special set of pads or keys that can trigger drum sounds, sound effects, guitar riffs, or other sounds to spice up the music. Different companies use different names for these pads, e.g., *multipads, touch pads, touch keys*, or *session partner pads*.

## Bass drums and timbales

On most keyboards you can play a host of percussion instruments by using the regular keys. Available sounds range from bass drums, snaredrums, toms, hi-hats, and cymbals to timbales, bells, and congas. Small icons of these instruments are often pictured above or below the corresponding keys. You can usually store the rhythms that you create this way.

## Split

Want to play a double bass sound with your left hand and a flute with your right? No problem: Most instruments have a *split* feature that divides the keyboard into a lower (left hand) and an upper (right hand) section. You can choose a different voice for each section.

## Layer

If you want to blend, say, the sound of a piano with that of a string section, you can do so by simply stacking these sounds on top of each other. This feature is called *layer, layering, dual voice*, or *dual mode*.

## Effects

Both keyboards and pianos offer various effects that enhance the

**Tipcode KEYS-005**
*Layering allows you to play different sounds at the same time, as demonstrated in this Tipcode.*

**TIPCODE**

17

sound by adding warmth and spaciousness, creating echoes, and so on. Two of the most common effects are *reverb* and *chorus*. Reverb makes you sound as if you're playing in a big hall or a church, rather than at home. Chorus is an effect that makes instruments sound fuller — as if you hear a choir (a chorus) singing, rather than a single voice.

### Pitch bend and modulation

Many digital keyboard instruments have two wheels to the left of the keyboard itself.

- One is used for **pitch bends**, bending the notes up the way guitarists often do. (On keyboards you can bend them down as well!)

- The other one is the **modulation wheel**, which usually lets you add *vibrato* to the sound.

*Bend the pitch up (to the right) or down (to the left), or move the stick forward to add modulation (Roland).*

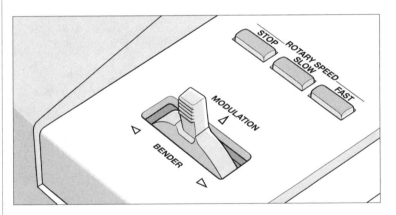

**Tipcode KEYS-006**
*Tipcode KEYS-006 demonstrates the use of pitch bend with various sounds.*

18

Some instruments have a joystick or another control that replaces both wheels.

### Synthesizer section

Various keyboards have a synthesizer section, allowing you to modify the available sounds to a certain extent. You can make them shorter or longer, or you make them go from soft to loud, for example.

### Sequencers

Most digital keyboard instruments allow you to record your own playing. The built-in recorder is usually referred to as a *sequencer.* It typically uses the same basic controls as a traditional recording device: record, pause, play, stop, fast forward, and rewind.

*This basic sequencer allows you to record and play back four songs.*

TIP

### Workstations and arrangers

*Keyboard makers use different names for their ranges of home keyboards, varying from interactive arrangers and arranger workstations to music workstations and performance controllers. There are no set definitions for these terms, though the word 'Workstation' typically indicates a higher level instrument with extended features. Chapter 12 deals with these and other keyboard family members.*

### New song, sounds, styles

It's often possible to provide your instrument with new sounds, songs, or styles, or to store your performances and other data. For this purpose, many of today's keyboards and pianos have a USB port to connect a USB memory stick or your compute; others (also) feature a card reader that allows you to read memory cards.

19

### Pedals on pianos
Most acoustic pianos have two pedals.

- Depressing the pedal on the right makes the sound sustain after you release the keys. This pedal is known as the **sustaining pedal or damper pedal**.

- The left pedal, which is usually called the **soft pedal**, lowers the volume and makes the sound a bit less bright.

Digital pianos need to have at least a sustaining pedal; some also have a soft pedal.

*Digital piano with damper and soft pedals (Yamaha).*

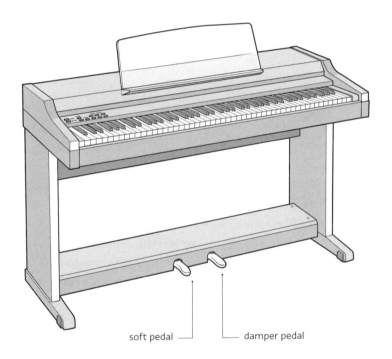

soft pedal ⎯⎯⎯  ⎯⎯⎯ damper pedal

### Pedals on keyboards
Most keyboards come without pedals. You can buy one or more of them as an option. A *volume pedal* or *expression pedal* is a popular choice, especially if you use a lot of organ sounds and electric guitar sounds. There are also *pedal switches* that you can use to control the accompaniment, for example (start, stop, variation, etc.).

20

*Continuous volume or expression pedal (left), and pedal switch.*

## Connections

The *connectors* for the instrument's pedals are usually located on the rear panel, together with one or more other connectors or *jacks*. Some examples:

- **Line out jacks** can be used to connect your instrument to an external sound system.

- **Line in jacks** allow you to have a CD player or another sound source play back through your main instrument's speakers.

- The **headphone jack** is usually located on the left side of the instrument, below the keyboard.

Chapter 8 discusses the connections in more detail.

*Rear panel of a keyboard, showing various inputs and outputs.*

## MIDI connections

One of the great features of keyboards and digital pianos is that you can hook them up to other instruments, or to your

21

computer. This way, you can use one keyboard to control various instruments, or you can use your computer as a digital recording studio, or you can use the Internet as an interactive tutor; the possibilities are endless. The system that allows you to do so is called MIDI. This *Musical Instrument Digital Interface* uses either special MIDI ports (in, out, and/or thru) or a USB port. Chapter 9 tells you more.

### Power

Most digital keyboard instruments operate at 9 or 12 volts DC; an adapter is required to convert the 110v or 230v current of the mains to this low voltage. Built-in adapters need to be shielded very well to prevent hum. Because of this and various other reasons it's much cheaper to supply an external adapter or offer one as an option, which is what most companies do. For onstage use, most musicians prefer an instrument with a built-in adapter for added operational safety. Some low-budget instruments run on batteries too.

### Other digital keyboard instruments

Many of the features mentioned here and elsewhere in this book can also be found on a host of other digital keyboard instruments. They all have MIDI, for example, and sequencers are just as common. Chapter 12 offers basic information on synthesizers, workstations, samplers, and related instruments.

# 3

# Learning to Play

Is it easy to learn to play a keyboard instrument? Yes
and no. Yes, because the layout of the keys makes the
keyboard very accessible. No, because you need to
get ten fingers to do exactly what you want them to,
which can be pretty hard. The best answer is that it all
depends on what you want to do.

If you've heard a tune somewhere, it's often easier to play it by ear on a keyboard instrument than on any other instrument. Why? Because one finger will do, and because all the notes are easy to find: higher notes to the right, lower ones to the left.

### Easy

Keyboards are among the easiest instruments to get started on: The instrument's auto accompaniment and chord recognition features do a lot of the work for you. However, learning how to play it really well requires as much musicianship and practice as any other instrument. In terms of learning to play, a digital piano is identical to an acoustic one.

### Two parts

What makes keyboard instruments different from most others is that you simultaneously play two parts: the melody with your right hand and the accompaniment with your left. On a piano, your left hand usually needs to do more than on a keyboard: Keyboards allow you to play chords with one or two fingers, and pianos don't.

### Reading music

Do you have to read music in order to play keyboard or piano? If you want to play classical music, the short answer is yes. If you're going to play anything else, then the answer is no, not necessarily. Still, being able to read music has a lot of advantages.

- It allows you to **instantly play new music** and communicate with other musicians that you may have never played with before.

- It gives you access to **loads of books and magazines** with exercises, songs, and solos.

- It provides you with **better insight** into the way chords, songs, and compositions are structured.

- It enables you to **put down on paper** your own songs, ideas, and exercises, both for yourself and for other musicians.

- It makes you **more of a musician**.

- It **widens the range of gigs** you can play, so it broadens your career options.

- Learning to read music **isn't that hard** at all. *Tipbook Music on Paper – Basic Theory* (see page 222) teaches you the basics within a few chapters.

- What's more, some keyboard instruments have features **to help you learn** how to read music, understand chords, and so on.

> ## Focus on the music
> When the time of the performance comes, just forget about the notes. You will play a lot better if you focus on the music instead of the notes. That's exactly why most keyboard players (including concert pianists!) don't use sheet music onstage.

### Taking lessons
Many digital instruments have educational features that help you learn to play, and you can find interactive keyboard lessons online as well. However, even the most advanced systems can't replace a 'real' teacher.

### A good teacher
More than how to read music and play the right notes, a good teacher will teach you about good technique, posture, dynamics, phrasing, and timing; how to interpret the music, what to study, or how to practice; how to use your talents and how to overcome your weak points, and so on. Just as important, your teacher provides you with personal guidance and feedback.

### Questions, questions
On your first visit to a teacher, don't just ask how much it costs. Here are some other questions:

- Is an **introductory lesson** included? This is a good way to find out how well you get on with the teacher and, for that matter, with the instrument.

**25**

- Will you be required to practice at least three hours a day, or can you also take lessons if you are just doing it **for the fun of it**?

- Do you need to buy a lot of books, or is **course material provided**?

- Is it possible to **record your lessons**, so you can go over the material again at home?

- Are you allowed to fully concentrate on **the style of music you want to play**, or will you be required — or encouraged — to learn other styles as well?

- Do you have to **practice scales** for two years, or will you be allowed to play songs as soon as possible?

- Is advice on **purchasing instruments** and other equipment included?

### Finding a teacher

Looking for a private teacher? Larger music stores may have teachers on staff, or they can refer you to one, and some players have found great teachers in musicians they have seen in performance. You can also find teachers online (see page 175). Alternatively, you may consult your local Musicians' Union, the band director at a high school in your vicinity, or check the classified ads in newspapers or music magazines. Professional private teachers will usually charge between twenty-five and seventy-five dollars per hour. Some make house calls, for which you'll pay extra.

### Music schools

You also may want to check whether there is a keyboard school, a teacher collective, or a music school in your vicinity. These organizations may offer extras such as ensemble playing, master classes, and clinics, in a wide variety of styles and at various levels.

### Group or individual lessons

You can take individual lessons, but you can also go for group lessons if that's an option in your area. Personal lessons are more expensive, but they can be tailored exactly to your needs.

# PRACTICING

How long you need to practice depends on what you want to achieve. Many great instrumentalists have practiced four to eight hours a day for years, or more. The more time you spend practicing (and playing!), the faster your playing will improve. Half an hour a day usually results in steady progress.

### The clock?
When it comes to practicing, however, you may wonder if it's wise to focus on the clock only. If you set yourself a goal instead ('At the end of this session, I want to be able to play this section without any mistakes', for example), you're focusing on the music – and that might well be more fun and inspire you to practice more!

### Headphones
One of the great advantages of playing an electronic instrument is that you can practice without bothering your neighbors or housemates. Just pop on some headphones or turn the volume down, and you can practice day and night.

### Piano?
If you want to learn to play the piano, it's best to practice on a digital or an acoustic piano. A piano teacher may not accept you as a student if you have a regular home keyboard instead. As explained in Chapter 2, they're quite different instruments.

### Keyboards
Keyboard teachers will often recommend that you have at least a 61-note instrument.

### Digital vs. acoustic
Even though digital pianos are getting to sound and feel more like acoustic ones, they're still not the same. You will have to make adjustments if you practice on one and have your lessons on the other.

27

### Practicing tools

Many digital keyboard instruments have one or more features that make practicing easier. For one thing, you can use the onboard sequencer to record the right-hand part of the music. Then play that back and practice the left hand along with the recording, at a tempo you can handle. Many instruments even offer a number of pre-recorded songs: You can have the instrument play one hand while you play the other. There's more about these and other options on page pages 90–91.

### Books, videos, DVDs, CDs

Besides a teacher, your instrument, and the Internet, there's even more material that can help you improve as a player.

- **Songbooks** contain transcriptions of songs that you can play.

- **Full accompaniments** for the songs you want to learn to play are available online.

- You can play along with **your favorite CDs**. This is even easier if your instrument has a special input for that purpose (see page 124).

- **Instructional videos and DVDs**, often created and presented by well-known musicians, can be very inspiring.

- **Keyboard magazines and websites** (see page 174–175) often publish useful playing tips, as well as transcriptions and exercises.

### Play a lot

Finally, one of the best ways to learn to play is seeing other musicians at work. Living legends or local amateurs — every concert or gig can be a learning experience. And the very best way to learn to play? Play a lot!

# 4

# *Buying an Instrument*

*You can get a keyboard for less than a hundred dollars, but that might not be the best choice if you're serious about making music. So how much should you spend, and what will that get you? Here are some basic considerations and useful pre-shopping tips.*

A decent entry-level keyboard that offers sufficient sound quality and the necessary features to keep you happy for a few years will typically cost you three hundred dollars or more. Most cheaper keyboards can be used to get acquainted with music, to help you with ear training, or just to fool around with, but they're usually not designed to suit the needs of aspiring musicians.

### Lots of everything

For three hundred dollars you have a choice of keyboards that look fairly spectacular, with an impressive amount of controls, hundreds of sounds, and a hundred different styles or more. So is there any sense in spending more?

### Three thousand and up

Yes, there is, as there's usually more than meets the eye. First of all, more expensive instruments usually sound better (see Chapter 6). They offer a greater range of sounds (Chapter 5) and accompaniments (Chapter 7). They feature more powerful sequencers (Chapter 5), more inputs and outputs (Chapters 8 and 9), and they often have a higher quality user interface (Chapter 5, again). A top-of-the-range keyboard may set you back three thousand dollars or more, without the optional pedals, hard disks, and other accessories.

### Digital pianos

Digital pianos, on average, are more expensive than keyboards. They usually have more keys (88) and a more complicated key mechanism, higher quality samples, and a better and more powerful sound system to realistically reproduce piano sounds. Some even have a wooden cabinet.

### Piano prices

Digital stage pianos with an 88-note hammer action keyboard start around five hundred dollars. 'Traditional' digital pianos are usually more expensive, due to their built-in sound system, among other things.

### Ensemble pianos

Digital ensemble pianos (featuring auto accompaniment,

numerous sounds and more) usually start around fifteen hundred dollars. Prices of digital grand pianos range from five to fifteen thousand dollars and more.

### Acoustic or digital?

Though digital pianos are getting closer and closer, they're still not identical to acoustic instruments. One major difference is that a digital piano uses loudspeakers to make the air vibrate, while an acoustic piano has a large wooden soundboard to amplify the vibrations of the strings. This is just one of the main reasons why many pianists — especially the ones who play classical music — will always prefer an acoustic instrument. That said, the Kawai company introduced a digital piano with both speakers and a wooden soundboard in 2007.

### Acoustic

Acoustic pianos are generally more expensive than their digital counterparts. They also need to be tuned at least twice a year, they need maintenance, and changes in humidity and temperature can affect their performance. They're also difficult (read: expensive) to move. Most acoustic pianos are considerably larger than digital models, though the required amount of floor space is about the same.

### Both acoustic and digital

The strengths of both acoustic and digital pianos are combined

### Resale value

Apart from subjective differences in sound and feel, acoustic pianos have the advantage that they can last a lifetime, and they retain most of their value if they're well maintained. Digital pianos don't. Though you can enjoy a good digital instrument for many, many years, the resale value drops considerably as soon as you leave the store. Why? Because new models are being launched every year, with even more sounds and more features, while the acoustic piano hasn't changed much in the past decades.

31

in a *hybrid piano*: an acoustic instrument with an onboard sound module (see page 159).

## SHOPPING

If you have decided to get yourself a keyboard or a digital piano, go visit friends and neighbors who own one. Ask if you can play their instrument, and find out how you like it. Experienced users can also shed light on the usefulness (or uselessness) of certain features.

### Shop around

Don't just buy from the first shop that happens to stock what you want, unless you fall head over heels in love with a certain instrument — and even then it may be a good idea to wait. Spend some time shopping around. Listen to a variety of instruments, and listen to a variety of sales people; they all have their own 'sound' as well.

### Make notes

It's hard to remember every detail of every instrument that you see or try out. Take notes of their most important features and of your findings as you play them, so you can keep track of what you're doing. Or do it the other way around: Make a list of everything you want your instrument to do (reading this book will help you compile this list), and ask the sales staff which models fit the bill.

**TIP**

### Demo

*Avoid sales staff who restrict their input to hitting the demo button. Also remember that it will take quite some time to learn to play the instrument as well as the one who performed the demo music. Demos are first and for all meant to sell you the instrument. So try not to be impressed by the dazzling display of technique and effects you commonly get to hear, but use the demo to carefully listen to how the instrument sounds.*

32

### A little more

Once you have your eye on an instrument, take one more look at the next model on the price list. Some fifty or a hundred dollars more may buy you useful features such as editable effects, pitch bend, modulation, or simply a better sound.

### A good store

Buying musical instruments is mostly a matter of comparing their sounds. You can do so only if you can play a few different instruments in the same room, on the same day. A good store offers sufficient stock and plenty of time to play-test instruments, as well as personal advice.

### Online and mail-order

Buying online or by mail-order makes it impossible to compare sounds, styles, the feel of the keys, the user interface, etc. That said, these companies usually offer a return service for most or all of their products: If you're not happy with your purchase, you can send it back within a certain period of time. Of course the instrument should be in new condition when you do.

### Depreciation

As technology progresses, home keyboards in particular tend to depreciate rapidly. They can lose up to eighty percent of their value within two or three years. The sunny side? Electronic instruments are frequently sold at bargain prices to make room for the latest models.

# USED INSTRUMENTS

Pre-owned digital instruments are available at very modest prices. Here are a few more things to think about.

### The very latest

Older instruments won't have all the latest music styles onboard, simply because these styles weren't around at the time the

keyboard was built. This is no problem if the instrument can be updated (see page 89).

### Privately or from a store?

Purchasing a used instrument from a private party may be cheaper than buying the same one from a store. One of the advantages of buying used instruments in a store, though, is that you can go back if you have questions: Good advice and service are often invaluable where musical instruments are concerned. Also, some music stores may offer you a limited warranty on your purchase. Another difference is that a good dealer won't usually ask an outrageous price, but private sellers might — because they don't know any better, or because they think that you don't.

## ANYTHING ELSE?

It's always a good idea to bring along an experienced keyboard player, maybe your teacher, when you go out shopping, particularly when buying a pre-owned instrument. Two see and hear more than one, even if you have learned this book by heart.

### Catalogs, magazines, and the Internet

Catalogs, brochures, and the Internet can provide you with detailed information outlining the differences and similarities between a wide variety of models and their features. Various magazines and websites offer reviews of the latest gear and plenty of additional information (see page174–175).

### Fairs and conventions

Visit music trade fairs, demo sessions, clinics, and music conventions if and when you can. Besides finding a considerable number of instruments to can try out and compare, you will also meet lots of knowledgeable product specialists and inspiring fellow musicians.

# 5

# A Good Instrument

They may all look pretty much the same, but they're not.
Both keyboards and digital pianos can differ widely in
quality and capabilities. This chapter deals with most
of the features that you can more or less judge without
playing a single note.

The information in this and the following chapters is meant to help you select an instrument, and to help you understand the instrument you have. Chapter 6 deals with sound, while auto accompaniment systems are covered in Chapter 7. Chapter 8 explains the various types of connections you may come across, and Chapter 9 is about MIDI.

# THE KEYS

The quality of the keyboard determines for a large part how easy it is to control the sound, and how much fun it is to play the instrument.

### Piano keyboards
Most digital pianos have 88 keys, just like most acoustic pianos. Models with less keys (typically 76) are easier to transport. Some pianos are available with either 88 of 76 keys; the latter can cost up to some 30 percent less.

### Classical music or jazz
Though most piano repertoire can be played on 76 keys, it is generally recommended to get an 88-note piano if you want to play classical music or jazz. In other styles of music, you will rarely miss the twelve extra keys that an 88-note keyboard offers.

TIP

> ### Extra keys
> *Compared to a 76-note keyboard, a keyboard with 88 keys has seven lower and five higher sounding extra keys.*

### C1 to C8
All 88-note instruments have eight C keys. The lowest one, on the far left, is called C1; the highest is C8. The notes in-between have corresponding numbers, e.g., the A above C4 is A4.

### Home keyboards: five octaves

Most serious keyboards are five-octave instruments, sporting 61 keys. Some have 76, and a few are available with either 61or 76 keys. As you can make the entire instrument sound one or more octaves higher or lower, a 61-note keyboard allow you to play both the very highest and the very lowest notes (transposing; see page 69). Having more keys at hand, however, gives you direct access to a larger range of notes.

### The same range

Instruments with an identical number of keys usually cover the same range (see the illustration below), except for those with 73 keys: Some 73-note keyboards go from E1 to E7, others from F1 to F7, or from C1 to C7.

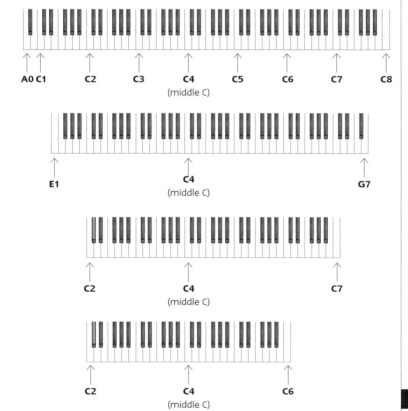

88-, 76-, 61-, and 49-note keyboards.

37

### Key shape

White keys come in various shapes. Most keyboard and synthesizers have *overhanging* or *synth-type* keys. Digital pianos usually have *piano-style* keys, also known as *box-type* keys.

### Waterfall

A third type of key, the *square-front* or *waterfall* key can be found on Hammond organs (see pages 154–155) and various instruments that emulate that type of sound. Waterfall keys look like piano-style keys without the small protruding lip at the front. They're usually combined with black keys with rounded off fronts. This design is best for playing glissandos, smearing your hand across the keys from left too right, or vice versa. These *glisses* are harder to do on synth-type keys, which can easily catch your skin.

*Square-front or waterfall keys (l), piano-style or box-type keys, and synth-style or overhanging keys (r).*

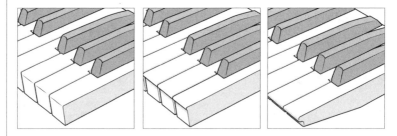

### Hammer action

On acoustic pianos, the keys trigger felt-tipped hammers to hit the strings. As the hammer hits a string, a damper moves away from it. When you let go of the key, the damper returns to the string. These moving hammers and dampers give the instrument its characteristic playing action. To emulate this type of action, most digital pianos have a key mechanism that includes a small hammer whose only purpose is to emulate the desired 'acoustic' feel. This type of mechanism is commonly known as a (*weighted*) *hammer action*, *hammered action*, or *piano-action* keyboard.

### Synth-action

Keyboards, synthesizers, and organs have *synth-action* or *non-weighted* keys. Contrary to piano-action keys, they use springs to return to their original position.

38

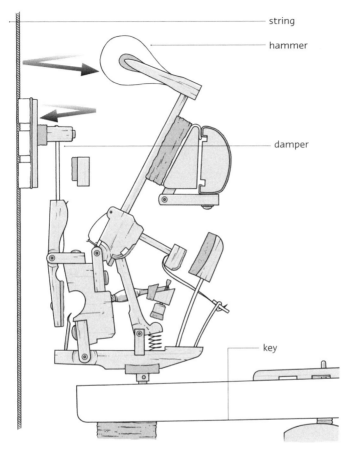

string

hammer

damper

key

The hammer mechanism in an acoustic piano. The downward motion of the key simultaneously makes the hammer hit the string and releases the damper. On releasing the key, the damper falls back into place, muting the string.

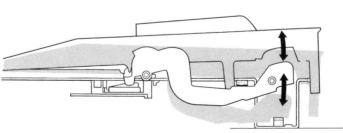

Hammer action. The hammer, just beneath the key, helps to mimic the action of an acoustic piano.

## The difference

Hammer action keyboards are heavier to play and require more practice and finger strength, but they provide more control over the tone and allow for expressive playing, just as acoustic pianos

**39**

do. If you're a pianist, a synth-action keyboard will feel kind of soggy or toy-like; if you're used to a synth-action keyboard, a piano-action will feel heavy and stiff, but you can get used to playing both.

### Wooden keys and more

To mimic the feel of an acoustic piano as best as possible, digital pianos often have balanced wooden keys, which provide an even feel all along the keyboard. Some also imitate the feel of other parts of the acoustic piano mechanism, such as the *let-off* or *escapement*. And as the lower notes of the acoustic instrument use heavier hammers and dampers than the higher ones, a growing number of digital instruments also emulate that effect, which is known as *scaled hammer effect* or *graded hammer action*.

### Semi-weighted keys

A *semi-weighted* keyboard has keys that feel heavier than those of a synth-action keyboard, but they don't imitate acoustic piano keys. If you don't like the 'floppy' or heavy feel of a hammer-action keyboard or the light keys of a synth-type keyboard, this might be what you're looking for.

**TIP**

> ### Confusing
> You may find the term 'weighted keyboard' to be used for what's described above as a semi-weighted keyboard, while others use it to indicate a hammer-action keyboard.

### The feel

When you compare instruments, you'll find that the key action may feel very different from one keyboard to another, or from one piano to another: Light or heavy, fast or sluggish, precise or lumpy, etc. What's best has as much to do with quality as with your preferences or your style of playing. Always turn on the instrument before checking the feel of the keys: They won't 'feel' good (and they're all too noisy) when there's no sound. Also check the keys for an even response all along the keyboard.

### Touch sensitivity

Almost every digital keyboard instrument is *touch sensitive*: The harder you hit the keys, the louder the sound will be. When you play harder, you actually move the keys down faster. It is this velocity (speed) that is measured and translated into a louder or a softer sound. This explains why this feature is also referred to as *velocity sensitivity*.

> ### Not just louder
>
> As you hit an acoustic piano key harder, the sound not only becomes louder, but a bit brighter too. Guitars, violins, and most other instruments respond in a similar way. High-quality keyboard instruments are capable of reproducing those subtle changes (see page 97).

### Keyboard touch response

On many pianos you can set the keyboard touch response, adapting the degree of sensitivity to your playing style. If you set it to *light* or *soft*, you don't need a pianist's technique to produce loud notes. The *hard* or *heavy* setting will give you the widest dynamic range, from a whisper to a roar. The number of settings or *velocity curves* varies from three to more than a hundred. On some, you can also design and store your personal touch curve. This won't alter the action: It just changes the way the keys respond to your playing.

### Harpsichords and organs

A number of traditional acoustic keyboard instruments, such as harpsichords and organs, are not touch sensitive. If you want to truly reproduce such instruments, you need to able to disengage the touch sensitivity feature. In some cases this happens automatically when you select one of these sounds. If so, you need a volume pedal (see page 49) to be able to vary the loudness of your organ sounds.

### Aftertouch

Some instruments offer a second stage of touch sensitivity that kicks in once the key has been depressed. This is known as

41

*aftertouch*. By pushing the key down a little further, you add a little extra color or volume to the sound, or another layer, vibrato (modulation), or pitch bend, for example. The effect may depend on the instrument, on the chosen sound (some instruments select an effect that works best for the sound you play), or on your settings.

### Channel or polyphonic
Few instruments have *polyphonic aftertouch*, meaning that only the pressed note is affected. This requires one pressure sensitive sensor per key. *Channel aftertouch* has one sensor for the entire keyboard, so all currently sounding notes will be affected.

### Release velocity
An instrument with *release velocity* is also sensitive to how quickly you let the keys go. This allows you to fade out strings gently as you bring up the keys, rather than cutting them off, for example.

### Multipads
On many keyboards, sounds can also be triggered by a series of *multipads*. Hitting these pads often activates drum, percussion, or effect sounds, but it can also trigger fill-ins or backing phrases (a horn section or a guitar riff to salt the accompaniment, for example), or even pre-arranged solos. Not all multipads or *touch pads* are touch sensitive.

*Multipads.*

### Assignable pads
On a growing number of instruments you can assign or *map* sounds, effects, or phrases to the pads. It may also be possible to use the pads to access other functions, such as selecting a pre-programmed style or sound, or turn on an effect for a solo.

42

# CONTROLLERS

Every digital keyboard instrument has a variety of controllers, ranging from knobs and sliders to wheels and joysticks.

### Fixed or assignable
The volume control is usually a *fixed function control*: You can't assign it to do anything else than adjusting the volume. Many controllers on keyboards perform more than one function. If you can assign a variety of functions to a controller yourself, you're dealing with an *assignable controller*.

### Faders
A *fader* is a sliding controller. Quite often, one fader is used to perform various functions, such as setting effects, adjusting tempo, or selecting a time signature (e.g., $\frac{4}{4}$ or $\frac{6}{8}$).

### Rotary controllers
These and many other functions can also be controlled by *rotary controllers* or *endless controllers*, i.e., controllers that can be rotated endlessly, rather than from 1 to 10. If a value has been set to 48, for example, and you turn the relevant controller up, it will start at 48 and increase the value from there.

### Soft keys
Both cell phones and home keyboards use *soft keys*. The function of these keys changes according to the software-driven information shown on the display. On keyboards, they can be used for a number of different things, from selecting sounds to setting effects. An illustration is shown on page 59.

### Touch screen
Many instruments feature a *touch screen* or *touch panel display*, allowing you to make selections by touching virtual 'buttons' that are displayed on the screen. Screen response time may vary from one instrument to the other. Some are quite slow, so you may want to check this when trying out instruments.

### Pitch bend and vibrato

Two of the most widely used effects are pitch bend and vibrato (typically referred to as modulation). You'll find them on most serious keyboards and some pianos. Many instruments have a *wheel controller* for each function.

• The wheel that controls **pitch bend** is usually self-centering: It jumps back as soon as you let go of it, returning to normal pitch.

• The wheel that controls **modulation** has to be returned to its 'neutral' position by hand.

• If there's a joystick that controls **both** pitch bend (moving it sideways) and modulation (moving it away from you), it's commonly self-centering for both effects.

*Joystick (left); pitch-bend and modulation wheels (right).*

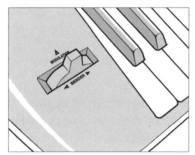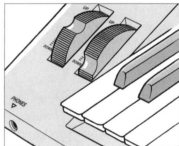

### Pitch bend

Pitch bend is essential if you want to play realistic guitar or wind instrument parts, for example. The degree of pitch bend is often programmable. Though typically set to bend up or down one whole step, you may be able set it to going up and down as much as an octave or more.

### Vibrato

For most keyboard players, the term modulation has grown to mean vibrato (a rapid pitch variation). Turning the modulation wheel up or moving the joystick away from you will increase the depth of the effect. Vibrato is essential to playing realistic string and wind instrument sounds.

**44**

> ## Modulation effects
> There are many effects that fit the term modulation effects, such as tremolo (amplitude modulation, i.e., varying the volume level), chorus, flanger, and phaser (see page 79). Vibrato is a pitch modulation or pitch variation.

**TIP**

### Other effects
Some keyboards allow you to assign other effects or functions to the modulation wheel, ranging from volume control to filters (see page 85), wah-wah effects, tremolo, and more.

### Ribbon controllers
On some instruments, you can control pitch bend, modulation, and other effects with a *ribbon controller* or *touch controller*. Sliding your finger over the ribbon bends the pitch up, or it increases vibrato depth, for example.

### Infrared light
Many buildings have doors that automatically open as you approach. Some keyboards have a similar feature, commonly known as a *beam controller*. By moving your hand through an invisible beam of infrared light, you can control a variety of effects and functions. You can bend the pitches you play, start or stop parts or all of the accompaniment, slow down or speed up the tempo of the song, add modulation to the sound, and so on.

### Breath control
Some instruments feature *breath control*. This allows you to control wind instrument sounds by breath pressure, varying the loudness by blowing harder or softer.

### Real-time controllers
Pitch-bend and modulation wheels, ribbons, and beam or breath controllers are perfect examples of *real-time controllers*: You can use them to change settings in real time, while you play. This makes for much more expressive and natural performances.

**45**

### Drawbars

Drawbars are best known from the Hammond tone wheel organs, which are portrayed on pages 154–155. When using organ sounds, these sliders add higher and lower *overtones* or *harmonics* to the notes you're playing. This imitates the effect of using *organ flutes* of various lengths (see page 153) that determine the exact timbre of an organ sound. If you use the 16' drawbar, it is as if you add the sound of a 16-foot organ flute to the note you play. This drawbar produces a note that sounds one octave below the pitch you are playing.

TIPCODE

**Tipcode KEYS-007**
*Drawbars are used to add harmonics to the tone, as you can clearly hear in this Tipcode.*

*Drawbars are used to add harmonics to the sound.*

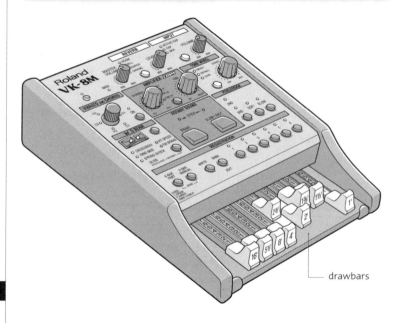

drawbars

### High and low

The 8' drawbar represents the actual note you are playing: If you push it in, you don't hear that pitch anymore. Pulling the 4 drawbar open adds the pitch of the first overtone of the note you play. This overtone sounds an octave higher. Opening the 2 ⅔ drawbar adds the second overtone, a fifth above the first one.

### Shorter but bassier

Though the 5 ⅓' drawbar adds a higher frequency to the note you play (after all, it is shorter than 8'), it actually tends to make for a fuller, bassier sound.

### Adding harmonics

The table below shows what the drawbars do when you play the note C4 (Middle C). Adding harmonics makes for a broader, richer sound, as you can easily hear.

| Drawbar | Overtones | Pitches |
|---------|-----------|---------|
| 16' | Subharmonic | C3 |
| 5 ⅓' | fifth above fundamental | G4 |
| 8' | Fundamental | C4 |
| 4' | first overtone | C5 |
| 2 ⅔' | second overtone | G5 |
| 1 ⅗' | fourth overtone | E6 |
| 1 ⅓' | fifth overtone | G6 |
| 1' | seventh overtone | C7 |

*Drawbars and overtones. The third column shows the generated pitches when playing middle C (C4).*

### Controllers

*Checking out the controllers themselves can give you an impression of the overall build quality of the instrument. Feel how they work and check knobs, switches, and wheels for play. They should only move in the intended direction. Some instruments have countersunk controls, which are less likely to snap off when you carry the instrument around or put it in a gig bag.*

TIP

### Virtual drawbars

Many keyboards have *virtual drawbars*. Their settings, usually adjustable by soft keys, are shown on-screen. Other designs use LEDs to show the settings for each drawbar, and up/down buttons to control them.

# PEDALS

Pedals can be used to perform a host of different functions.

### Pedals for pianos

In an acoustic piano, the sustaining pedal or damper pedal is used to move the dampers from and to the strings. The pedal mechanism lets you control how fast this happens, and you can vary the distance between dampers and strings. Good digital pianos allow you to perform these *half pedal techniques* and other pedal techniques, which all require a *continuous pedal*. A single, continuous piano-style pedal will typically cost you some twenty-five to fifty dollars.

### Switch

Cheaper instruments sometimes use a footswitch that allows for dampers on or off only. Note that there are continuous pedals that look like the footswitch pictured below.

*A continuous piano-style pedal and a footswitch or pedal switch.*

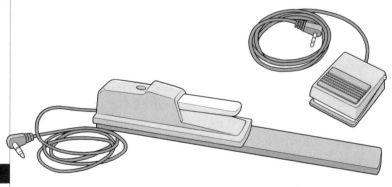

## On the left

On acoustic pianos, the left pedal (piano pedal or *soft pedal*) brings the hammers closer to the strings, reducing the volume and producing a softer tone. Digital pianos emulate this effect electronically. Serious pianists need this pedal, which is often combined with a damper pedal in one unit.

## In the middle

Many upmarket digital pianos have a third, middle pedal, known as the *sostenuto pedal*. Play a chord, then depress the pedal; the chord will be sustained, while any further notes you play won't. This pedal is required for a limited number of classical compositions only, but it can be used for pianistic effects in other styles as well, of course. A piano with three pedals is shown on page 52.

### Bach

Some of the works of Johan Sebastian Bach require the use of a sostenuto pedal, which explains why it's also known as a Bach pedal. Yet another name is Steinway pedal: Steinway, the well-known piano maker, acquired the patent on the original sostenuto pedal invented by the French piano company Pleyel in 1875.

## Volume pedal

The organ is not a touch sensitive instrument. Instead, you use a *volume pedal* or *expression pedal* to control the volume. Keyboards gain a lot of expressiveness when you add such a pedal to your rig. You can use it to make guitars and wind instruments sound much more convincing as well.

### Continuous pedal

A volume pedal or expression pedal is a continuous pedal, just like a proper piano pedal. A continuous pedal allows you to alter a parameter (such as volume) continuously over a certain range, other than an on/off switch.

**49**

### Pedal versus touch sensitivity

Controlling the volume with a pedal has a different effect than using the keyboard's touch sensitivity: The pedal controls the overall volume, while touch sensitivity allows you to control the volume from key to key. Of course you can use touch sensitivity when playing organ sounds, but it doesn't make for a natural organ sound. Likewise, it would not be natural to play a piano chord and then make the volume go up using a pedal — but that doesn't mean it can't be fun to do so.

### Prices

You can get a volume pedal for less than thirty dollars, but top of the range models (sporting a minimum volume knob and other features) may cost a hundred and fifty or more.

### Multiswitch

Also available are (*MIDI*) *foot controllers* or *multiswitches* with as many as ten or more assignable switches that allow hands-free operation of a variety of tasks (start, stop, next sound or style, fill, ending, etc.). Some also include a continuous pedal. Depending on the quality and the number of switches or pedals and what they can do, such units usually cost anywhere from one to four hundred dollars.

### Pedal connections

Basic keyboards may have room for a single pedal only (usually allowing for a continuous damper or expression pedal, or an assignable switch); more advanced models offer more connections.

*Bass pedal or pedal keyboard.*

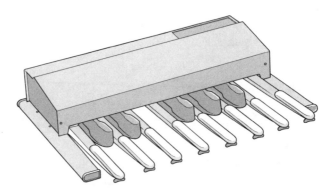

An *assignable pedal* input allows you to choose what you want the pedal to do: change volume level, control 'dampers,' select the next sound or style, and so on. Note that some instruments require specific multiswitches or pedals.

### Bass pedals

Keyboards may have an input jack for a *bass pedal board* with up to some thirty oversized keys, on which you can play bass parts with your feet, just like conventional organ players do. Some of these pedals can be used to play harmonies, drums, or percussion sounds as well, or to trigger effects or control MIDI functions (see Chapter 9). Bass pedal boards are also known as *pedal claviers* or *pedal keyboards.*

### Rugged and non-slip

If you want to use a pedal onstage, go for one that's rugged enough to withstand some abuse. It should have a non-slip bottom too.

# THE HOUSING

If you plan to play your instrument in your living room, looks will probably play a role in your selection. For instruments that are going to be used onstage, solidity and weight will be more relevant.

### Stage pianos

Higher quality stage pianos often have a rugged metal chassis, which makes the instrument both road-tough and quite heavy. Professional stage pianos easily weigh fifty pounds or more.

> **Matching stand**
>
> Some portable keyboards and digital pianos come with an optional matching stand. A few companies make matching stands with built-in piano-style pedals for some of their instruments.

TIP

**51**

### Keyboards
Keyboards are considerably lighter. This makes them easier to handle but they're also quite vulnerable. If you take any keyboard instrument on the road, make sure to pack it in a good bag or case (see pages 145–146).

### Music rest
Onboard music rests come in a lot of different guises, varying from plasticized wire frames that can be clipped onto the instrument to heavily sculptured designs. They're not always included.

### Spinets and consoles
Most upright digital pianos look more or less like small upright acoustic *spinet pianos* (up to some forty inches or one meter high) or slightly larger *console* or *studio* pianos (up to about forty-five inches; 115 cm).

### Grand pianos
Digital grand pianos are generally smaller than acoustic models. Their sizes range from around 27.5" (68cm) to 5'9" (175 cm). Acoustic grand pianos range from some 5' (150 cm) for a *baby grand* to 9' (275 cm) or even more for a *concert grand piano*.

*Spinet-size piano with sustain pedal (r), sostenuto pedal (center) and soft pedal (l).*

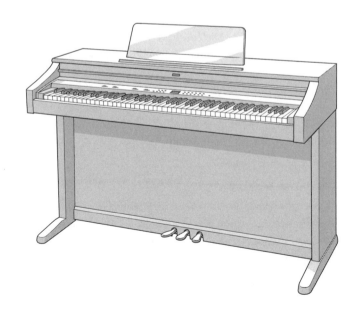

### Single panel or sound box

Most digital pianos have a single panel under the keyboard, as shown below. Other models have a large 'sound box' instead, making them look more like an acoustic instrument.

### Real wood vs. wood-grain

Very few digital pianos feature a real wood cabinets. Most use MDF or similar materials, covered with a *wood-grain* or *simulated wood* finish, or a thin ply of real wood (*veneer*). Some companies claim that a wood construction enhances the sound, making it warmer and more natural. The same goes for acoustic pianos, incidentally.

### The more you pay

The more you pay, the more your digital piano will usually look like a conventional acoustic instrument, with brass plated pedals and caster wheels, a sculptured music rack, a matching bench, and so on. Modern designs are also available.

### Bigger

Bigger instruments often — but not always — sound better because they house bigger and better speakers, and appropriate amplification.

### Finishes

Both wood and wood-grain instruments come in a wide variety of finishes, from rosewood and gloss mahogany to cherry, polished ebony, and Mediterranean oak satin.

### Weight

Full cabinet digital pianos are easier to handle and to move than their acoustic cousins, yet they can be quite heavy, up to three some three hundred pounds (135 kilos). Digital grand pianos can be even heavier.

### Benches

Some digital pianos come with a matching bench or offer one as an option. Height adjustable benches are available for as little as fifty dollars. Spending more may get you more comfortable

53

cushioning, infinite height adjustment (seriously to be considered if various people use the instrument), a sheet music compartment below the seat, and legs with leveling adjusters that keep the bench from wobbling on uneven floors.

*Basic height-adjustable, collapsible bench.*

# DISPLAYS

The display keeps you informed about what you (and your instrument) are doing. There are two basic display types: numeric and LCD.

### Numeric
A *numeric display* is usually limited to showing a few numbers or letters, presenting information in an abbreviated form. For example, T112 would mean that the tempo (T) is set at 112 *beats per minute* (*bpm*), while SO34 would indicate that you're using sound (SO) number 34. You may still find this type of display on very low-budget (or old) keyboards, and on digital pianos with a very limited number of features. In fact, some digital pianos don't have a display at all.

**54**

*A numeric display.*

## Liquid Crystals

Most digital instruments have a graphic display, similar to a cell phone display, known as an *LCD* (*Liquid Crystal Display*). On keyboards and ensemble pianos, the display shows a host of information, ranging from the selected sounds, tempo, and style, to the chords, the keys and the notes you're playing, volume and effect settings, and so on.

## Larger display

A larger display usually provides simultaneous access to a lot of information, it has room for larger, easier-to-read type and graphic icons, and it's less likely to use puzzling abbreviations such as vRomtcTp (a vibrating trumpet sound!).

*A display showing the accompaniment, the tempo, the effects and sounds that are being used, and more.*

## Pixels

The number of pixels, often specified in seductive phrases like 'large 320x240 display,' doesn't tell you anything about the physical size of the display. If you have two equally sized displays,

55

the one with the higher pixel count has a higher resolution, meaning that it produces a more defined image.

### Color

On full-color displays, the colors can be used to enhance the presentation and organization of the information. For example, some screens change color to indicate the current mode (style, song, record, and so on).

> ## Adjustable angle
>
> The visibility of the display can be improved if its angle is adjustable — which rarely is the case. Some of these displays lock flat for easier transportation.

### Visibility

A *contrast control* helps to improve the readability of the display under various lighting conditions. If it gets really dark, you will need a backlit display. Some instruments have illuminated buttons as well. If the display lights up only if you're operating the controls of the instrument (similar to cell phones, again), it doesn't distract you when you're playing. A few instruments have sockets that allow you to connect a gooseneck lamp.

*... sheet music and lyrics advance as you play...*

### Sheet music and lyrics

Some instruments can also display sheet music and lyrics (see page 76), which advance as you play. Instruments that feature a karaoke system often allow you to connect a TV or another type of monitor so others can sing along (i.e., *multimedia keyboards*). The required video interface may be included or optional. Others also offer the possibility to display a slide show of your digital images, or even video.

# USER-FRIENDLINESS

The way the information is organized on the display is a major factor in how user-friendly an instrument is, but there's more.

### High button count

A high button count may look intimidating, but it has its advantages. If the most common features have dedicated buttons, knobs, or faders, they're easier to access than having a limited number of buttons that you need to press seven times before you reach the option that you want.

### Without the manual

Menus and submenus should be well-organized. Ideally, you should be able to make the instrument do everything you want it to without using the manual — but very few instruments are that user-friendly. Advanced instruments often provide a *help* function.

### User-friendly?

What else makes an instrument more user-friendly?

- A well-organized **layout** of the controls.

- A number of buttons that you can **program** to memorize your favorite sounds and styles.

- **A help tool**, triggered perhaps by pressing the relevant button for longer than two seconds.

57

- An **intuitive way** to go from one screen to the other (and back!)

- **Vocal cues** that announce functions.

- **A panic or exit button** that allows you to go back to the previous menu or the instrument's home page.

- A display that offers the relevant information as soon as you **activate a certain function**.

- The possibility to choose **your own language**, other than English (some speak as many as six!)

# SELECTING SOUNDS AND STYLES

There are many different systems for selecting sounds and accompaniments on keyboards. Pianos are typically easier to operate, so that's where this section starts.

### Two at a time

Pianos with a limited number of sounds usually have a dedicated button for each available sound. Voices can often be layered by simply pushing two buttons at a time.

### Groupings

On keyboards and (ensemble) pianos that feature lots of sounds, the sounds are usually grouped into *banks*, *sound families*, or *sound categories*. Each group contains a number of related sounds: pianos in group one, chromatic or melodic percussion (vibraphone, glockenspiel, etc.) in group two, organs in group three, guitars in group four, and so on.

### Accompaniments

Accompaniments are usually grouped by style: pop, Latin, jazz, dance, and so on, with each group containing a variety of patterns.

### Calling up sounds

Lower-budget instruments often list numbered sounds and styles on the front panel. You choose a style or sound by punching in the corresponding number on a numeric keypad, or by using button combinations. If the baritone saxophone is sound number 14 in group B, you simply push the buttons B, 1 and 4.

*Selecting sounds and accompaniments using a numeric keypad.*

## On display

If an instrument has more sounds and styles than can be printed on the front panel, you usually make your selections from the display, typically by using soft keys, or virtual controls on a touch screen.

*Soft keys allow you to find the desired guitar sound (GEM).*

*Data entry wheel.*

### Data entry wheel

Many instruments use a *data entry wheel* to scroll through sounds or styles. Data entry wheels, also known as *jog wheels* or *alpha dials*, are also used to select tempo, or to assign sounds to multipads, for example.

### Enter button

If you use a data entry wheel to select sounds and styles, you'll usually have to press an *enter button* to confirm your choice.

### Variations

Instruments often provide one or more variations on their sounds. Variations on a saxophone voice, for example, might include that same saxophone with a vibrato, or with a chorus. Some of these variations can be very subtle: a grand piano sample, for instance, with varying degrees to which the lid is opened (the display showing the corresponding lid angle!). In other cases, the variations are simply the voices of related instruments: an upright bass or double bass sound with an electric bass guitar and a fretless bass guitar as variations, for example.

### Search engine

If you have hundreds of sounds or styles to choose from, a built-in *search engine* makes life much easier. Finding styles is facilitated if you can group them in various ways (e.g., musical style, era, alphabetical). On some instruments, you can find songs by playing the first few notes of the melody. These and many other features are getting more and more common.

**Demo per sound**

*A few instruments offer demos that illustrate the specific characteristics of each voice individually. This can be of great help when selecting sounds, or getting to know each voice and its possibilities.*

### Direct piano

The acoustic piano voice is still the single most popular sound, both on digital pianos and on keyboards. That explains why quite a lot of keyboards have a 'direct piano' or 'piano setting' button that activates the instrument's very best piano sound and puts the keyboard in the full mode (see page 116), so it can be played like a 'real' piano.

### One touch

Keyboards automatically match certain sounds or voices to the style you select: a tenor saxophone for a jazzy ballad, a trumpet

61

for salsa. Calling up that sound is a matter of pressing a button labeled *one touch* or *single touch*, for example. Appropriate effects and layers may be chosen automatically as well. Some instruments even provide you with two, three, or more matching instruments.

### One key, various sounds

With certain voices, there may be different samples under each key, for example, a jazz scat voice that triggers different scat sounds depending on how hard you hit the keys: '*du*,' '*dap*,' '*daooooow*'...

**TIPCODE**

**Tipcode KEYS-008**
This Tipcode demonstrates how you can play different tones or voices with just one key.

# SPLITS

When you use the split function, the two resulting keyboard sections are typically called *upper* and *lower*. This stems from the upper and lower keyboard or *manual* of so-called *dual manual organs* (see page 153). On these instruments, each manual or keyboard has its own (drawbar or register) settings.

**TIP**

### Double keyboard

*Wersi is a German company that makes keyboards in the organ tradition, with separate upper and lower keyboards.*

### Split point

On most instruments, you can set the split point yourself. This is known as a *floating* or *programmable split*. The note you select will usually be the lowest note for the upper (right hand) section.

### Multiple splits

Multiple splits are less common, but there are keyboards than you can divide into a number of zones, each with its own sound. These zones can then be assigned their own pitch as well (transposing, see page 69). This means that you can, for example, alternate between a sax and a trumpet, playing them at identical pitches in different areas of the keyboard.

### Balance

For a musical performance, it is important that you can adjust the volume level for each voice independently.

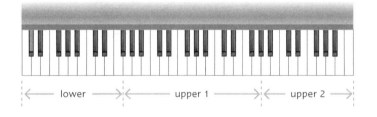

| ←——— lower ———→ | ←——— upper 1 ———→ | ←——— upper 2 ———→ |

Multiple
floating
splits

### Chord recognition

If you're using the chord recognition feature of a keyboard (e.g., *arranger mode*), you can usually determine where the split between the chord recognition area and the upper section occurs.

# LAYERS

With most instruments you can layer two sounds, and a few allow you to stack more sounds on top of that. The various voices of a layered sound in the upper part of the keyboard are usually labeled

63

*upper 1* or *upper orchestra 1*, *upper 2*, and so on. The lower half of the keyboard may have a layering option as well.

### Flexibility

The more layers you have available, the more flexible you can be in creating your own sounds. For instance, you could use four layers to make up your own horn section, either a traditional one, with a trumpet, an alto sax and two tenor saxes, or an alternative quartet of a soprano sax, a trombone and two tubas. Or you can use multiple layers to create a broad, fat-sounding string section by blending several string sounds at slightly different pitches.

### Separate buttons

Some instruments have a separate button for each sound you can select in a performance. This allows you to play all those sounds simultaneously by just pressing the corresponding buttons, or to switch from one sound to the other, so you can play call and response choruses by yourself: four bars sax solo, four bars guitar, four bars piano, back to the saxophone, and so on.

### Transpose

If you can transpose (see page 69) the sounds in a layer independently, you can create nice textures: Play a piano solo and let a string section play along a fifth higher, for example, or use two keyboard sounds for a fuller effect.

TIP

### Combinations

*Layers and splits can often be used in a wide variety of combinations. One example is to use the lower part of the keyboard for one sound, the upper part for another, and add strings to both.*

## VOLUME AND BALANCE

**64**

Layers, splits, and accompaniments bring a great number of volume levels into play. Ideally, the volume of each part or section should be independently controllable, just as it would be in a recording studio. The more sophisticated the instrument, the more independent volume controls will generally be available. For a musical performance, it helps if you're able to adjust the balances between the various sounds in a layer, between the lower and upper sections of a split keyboard, and between the accompaniment and the melody. A few instruments have *style touch sensitivity*, allowing you to control the volume of the accompaniment in real time, simply by how hard you play the chords in the lower section of the keyboard.

### Accompaniment balance

You may also be able to adjust the balance of the various *tracks* of the accompaniment. A typical arrangement has four volume controls marked *bass*, *drums*, *acc1*, and *acc2*. The sounds used for the parts labeled *acc1* and *acc2* can vary: a piano and a brass section in one style, or a funky guitar and strings in another, and so on.

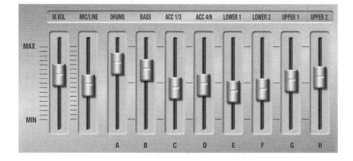

*Separate controls for master volume, microphone level, drums, bass, accompaniments 1 to 3, and so on.*

# TONE CONTROL

The amplifier of your home stereo has bass and treble controls that allow you to adjust the 'timbre' of the sound by boosting or cutting low and high frequency ranges. This is known as *equalization* or *EQ*. Most digital keyboard instruments have similar controls.

65

### Switch or fader

Lower priced pianos often have a *brilliance switch* with the settings *mellow* (reduced highs, boosted lows), *normal*, and *bright* (boosted highs, reduced lows). More expensive instruments typically feature a continuously adjustable brilliance control with a fader or up-down buttons, allowing for finer adjustment.

### Graphic equalizer

Another step up is a tone control with separate controls for a number of *frequency ranges* or *bands*. This is known as a *graphic equalizer*: It graphically shows you its settings. Graphic EQs are usually limited to mid- and pro-level instruments. Some keyboards even allow you to set the EQ per voice.

*An 8-band graphic equalizer. The band marked 63 (63 hertz) controls the lowest frequencies; the band marked 8K (8,000 hertz) controls the highest frequencies.*

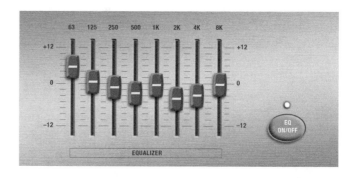

### Bass boost

Dance music often requires a fat, pumping bass sound, which some companies supply with features labeled *auto loudness* or *bass boost*, for example.

### Effect

Equalizers are usually considered effects. After all, they affect the timbre of the sound you produce. Other effects are covered on pages 79–81.

66

# TUNING

Digital keyboard instruments don't need to be tuned before you can play. However, you can adjust their tuning in various ways.

### Fine tuning

When you're playing in a band or along to a CD, your instrument may sound a little *flat* (too low) or *sharp* (too high). To adjust this, most keyboards and pianos can be fine-tuned. Usually, your keyboard will be tuned at the standard pitch A=440. This means that the key A4 (see page 36) produces a pitch of 440 vibrations per second, or 440 hertz. When you play this pitch on a guitar or a violin, the string will vibrate 440 times per second.

*Fine tuning the instrument in 0.5 hertz increments.*

**Tipcode KEYS-009**
*Most digital instruments can be fine-tuned over quite a wide range. Listen to this Tipcode.*

**TIPCODE**

67

## Increments

Most instruments can be tuned at least a quarter tone up and down (+ or –50 cents, i.e. from 427.5 to 452.5 Hertz). Increments of 1 hertz are acceptable; the smallest increment is 0.1 hertz. Fine-tuning is also known as master tuning.

### Quarter-tone intervals

When you go from one key to the next, you play *half-tone* or *semitone* intervals. In various non-Western styles of music (e.g., Middle Eastern and Arabic music) quarter-tone intervals are used as well. Some keyboards have preset tunings for these styles of music, in which, for example, D and A or E and B are lowered a quarter tone. Others have even more sophisticated features that allow you to play any type of scale with similar *microtunings*.

### Historical tunings

In Western music, several different tunings or *temperaments* have been used over the centuries. If you want to play the music of a certain era, it helps if you can play it with the proper tuning. Some instruments offer a choice of tunings for this purpose, from the thirteenth-century Pythagorean tuning to the eighteenth-century Kirnberger or Tartini Valotti tunings, as well as different modern piano tunings. One example of the latter would be *stretch tuning*, inspired by the perception that high notes sound too low (so they're tuned up a bit), and low notes sound too high (so they're tuned a little flat).

## Personal tunings

Two identical, perfectly tuned acoustic pianos can sound very different because of minute differences in the exact way they have been tuned. Some digital pianos can be tuned per key, so you can have your favorite piano tuner tune it for you that way you like it.

# TRANSPOSING

If the vocalist of the band can't sing the highest notes, you will have to play the entire song a number of steps lower. In other words, you need to *transpose* the song to *another key**. On acoustic instruments, this means that you'll have to use different keys, chords, and — thus — fingerings. On a digital instrument, you simply hit the transpose function. This makes all the keys sound any number of half steps higher or lower, and you can just play the chords you're used to.

*Transposing: In the position shown, each C key sounds the note D; each D key sounds the note E, and so on.*

### One or two octaves
Keyboards and pianos can often be transposed over a range of one or two octaves, sometimes even more. This feature also increases the range of your instrument: You can play higher and lower notes than the actual number of keys suggests. A tip: When you use the split function, you can usually independently transpose each section.

### Transposing and layers
If you can transpose one of the voices in a layered sound, you can play two-voiced harmonies using single keys only — a piano with a layered flute voice that sounds an octave higher, for example.

# POLYPHONY AND MULTITIMBRALITY

Early electronic instruments were *monophonic*: As with a sax or a trumpet, you could produce only a single (*mono*) note at a time.

*Tipbook Music on Paper *tells you everything about key signatures and transposing. See page 222.*

All modern keyboard instruments are *polyphonic,* so you can play a lot of notes simultaneously, like you can on a guitar or a piano. Most are also *multitimbral,* meaning that they can also produce different sounds (*timbres*) at once.

### Polyphony

For most applications, you will need an instrument with at least *24-note* or *24-voice* polyphony. Why, if you have ten fingers only? Because the accompaniment plays a lot of simultaneous notes too, for one thing. And when you use layered sounds, each note will use up as many voices as there are layers.

### On piano

On a piano you need multinote polyphony to play sustained chords, or *arpeggios* and glissandos while using the damper pedal, which may require dozens of notes to sound simultaneously. Beginning and intermediate pianists need 16- or 32-note polyphony at least, but professional pianos often have 64- or 128-note polyphony, or even more. Low polyphony can cause *note stealing* (notes being cut off when you play another note) or *attack flamming.*

### Multitimbral

A *16-part multitimbral* instrument is capable of having sixteen *different* sounds or voices going on at the same time. This may seem like a lot, but splits, layers, and accompaniments may eat up these parts faster than you think.

# REGISTRATION MEMORIES

On most instruments you can save your settings for each song (style, sounds, effects, transposition, tempo, volume levels, etc.) in *registration memories, registrations, panel storage settings, performance settings,* or *user programs.* These can be recalled at the touch of a button. Their number varies from four or six to a hundred or more.

### Pre-programmed settings

Some instruments have pre-programmed settings for hundreds of well-known songs. To prevent copyright problems, song titles may have been changed slightly (e.g., *Against All 'The' Odds*).

*Registration memories.*

# SEQUENCERS

A basic sequencer allows you to record just one or a few songs that you can play back, and that's it. A really powerful sequencer is almost like a digital recording studio that allows you to create multipart songs, recording each new instrument while playing back the ones your already recorded.

### No sound...

Sequencers do not record sound (like traditional — tape or CD — recorders do), but they digitally record the keys you press, the velocity at which you do so, the effects you use, the pedals you press, and so on.

### ... but events

Everything you do during a performance (pressing a key, releasing the key, setting the intensity of an effect, setting the tempo, using a pedal) is an *event*. A sequencer records these events as *MIDI messages* (see page 131). Playing back these data is like having a remote control operate the instrument.

### Number of events

The capacity of a sequencer is usually expressed as the number of events it can hold in memory, and sometimes as the number of notes. A 1,600-note song memory may sound impressive at first, but at a moderate tempo you play that many notes in a matter of minutes.

71

### Pianos and keyboards

For digital pianos, a capacity of 30,000 to 45,000 events is not unusual. Because they have to record the accompaniment parts as well, keyboards need larger memories. Top level keyboards may go up to 250,000 events or more.

TIP

---

### Data transfer

Initially, the capacity of these sequencers increased with every new generation of keyboards and pianos. With the arrival of USB ports — and thus the possibility to store recordings on computer hard disks or USB sticks — and memory cards, expanding their capacity became irrelevant: You can simply store your surplus of data elsewhere.

---

### Number of songs or measures

Sequencers also vary in the number of songs they can hold, ranging from one to 200 or more. Some companies also specify the maximum number of bars or measures for each song. Here's a guideline: At tempo 120 — a very common 'marching' tempo at two beats a second — a five-minute song in $\frac{4}{4}$ has 150 bars.

### Number of tracks

Very basic sequencers have one single track. You play, it records: end of story. If the sequencer has two tracks, you can usually play one back while recording the other. This allows you to record the left hand part first, for example, and then add the right hand part to it on the second track.

### Multitracking

The more tracks you have, the more complicated you can make your arrangements, through *multitracking*. Many instruments have an eight-track sequencer, while top-of-the-line models often sport 16, allowing you to add as many parts, sound by sound, part by part. A few instruments have dual sequencers that can be synchronized, so you can use all their tracks simultaneously.

72

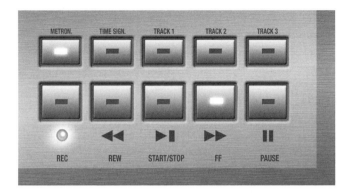

A three-track
sequencer with
the familiar
transport
controls.

### Resolution

Sequencers record events according to a grid. The finer this
grid, the more accurately the sequencer will reproduce the exact
timing of your notes. This grid is referred to as the instrument's
(*timing*) *resolution*. With a resolution of 48, there are 48 different
points at which a note can be recorded within each beat (usually
a quarter note). This isn't as accurate as it may sound. If you want
a true representation of your playing, the sequencer should have a
resolution of 96 or 192 *ppq* (*pulses per quarter note*).

### Quantizing

Sophisticated sequencers allow you to fix timing errors in your
performance. This is known as *quantizing* or *quantization*. If you
set the quantization to sixteenth notes, every poorly timed note
you play will be moved to the nearest sixteenth note.

---

### (Non-)volatile

Sequencers in entry-level instruments may memorize and
store your performance only until the instrument is switched
off. Most sequencers preserve their contents at power-off,
however: They have a non-volatile song memory.

---

### Editing

The degree to which a sequencer allows you to edit your recordings
varies per instrument. On some, you can just change the playback

73

tempo. On others, you may also be able to correct wrong notes, replace sounds, change the effect settings or EQ per sound, transpose the sequence, copy and paste parts of the song, layer sounds, and so on.

### Real time, step time

Most sequencers can record both in *real time* (you play, the sequencer records) and in *step time*. Step time recording is rather like programming, and it's usually a lot more complicated than real time recording. On the other hand, it allows you to record things you can't actually play!

### Your computer

If your instrument's sequencer isn't powerful enough, you can hook up your instrument to your computer and get a *software sequencer*: a piece of software that turns your computer into a sequencer. Software sequencers or *computer-based sequencers* usually have numerous editing options that allow you to store as many songs as you like. Most of these sequencers can record audio too, so you can add vocals and actual instruments to your recordings, which can then be burned onto a CD.

## STANDARD MIDI FILES

If you save a performance, it will commonly be stored as a *standard MIDI file*, also known as *MIDI file* or *SMF* (.mid).

### Formats

Depending on the instrument, the sequencer will use a certain SMF format. These formats (GM, GS, XG, and others) are briefly explained on page 140. They make sure that if you play back your performance on an instrument that can handle that format, you will hear the same notes and the same voices you played when recording the song, with the same effects and other setting.

### General MIDI

The GM (*General MIDI*) format is the only one that can be read and saved by sequencers of (almost) every brand. This explains why Standard MIDI files are often dubbed *General MIDI files.*

### Disk drive

MIDI files take up very little storage space: A song is usually no larger than 40K to 100K. (A CD-quality audio recording takes up about 10,000K (10MB) per minute! As MIDI files are that small, you can easily save a lot of 'music'.

### Songs

Most popular songs are available as Standard MIDI files, either commercially or free. You can simply download them online and use them to sing along to, to provide accompaniment for your solos, to practice playing them, or to just play them back and enjoy the music. If you want to sing along it can be helpful if your keyboard is capable of transposing the song to a key that matches your range (see page 69).

### Arranging and editing MIDI files

Provided that you have the right software, you can edit Standard MIDI files on your computer: change voices, effect levels, or velocities, transpose the song, and so on. Some keyboards allow you to arrange song files on the fly, so you can *loop* (endlessly repeat) the chorus as long as everybody's still dancing, for example.

### Files and styles

Some keyboards can combine Standard MIDI files with any style you want, so you can experiment and see which styles best fit your favorite songs.

### Add audio

*Provided with the right tools (software, instruments, microphones, an audio interface for your computer), you can also add audio to these MIDI files, ranging from vocals to acoustic guitar parts. Save the result as an MP3 file and use it for your one man band performance!*

75

### Various types

There are various types of Standard MIDI files: Type 0, Type 1, Type 2, and Type 1+lyrics.

- **Type 0** saves songs in a single track. As each part uses its own MIDI channel (see page 132), you can still edit the individual parts, provided you have the right equipment.

- **Type 1** uses a multitrack format, allowing you to adjust the volume of each part, for example.

- **Type 1+Lyrics** presents the lyrics of the song on your display, if your instrument can handle this format.

- **Type 2**, which is rarely used, can save multiple songs in a single file.

### Type 0

Some entry-level or older instruments can handle Type 0 only. Instruments that can read Type 1 can also read type 0. If you want to make sure that every instrument can read your MIDI files, save them as Type 0.

# SAMPLERS

Sampling is a feature that's usually reserved for high-end keyboards. With a sampler, you can make digital recordings — samples — of sounds, and add them to the voices in your instrument's memory. A sample can be a single sound or note, or a short phrase, a guitar riff, a drum loop, or whatever, recorded by using the microphone or line inputs of your instrument (see Chapter 8).

### Sample memory

The amount of sample memory determines the maximum length of a sample. As a guideline, a 16MB memory allows for a stereo sample of slightly under 90 seconds. Sample memory can usually be expanded with memory modules, similar to the way you can have the internal memory of your computer expanded.

76

### File formats

Samples are commonly saved as WAV files (for PC) or AIFF files (for Macintosh), so you can edit them on your computer. WAV and AIFF are not the only sample formats. Some companies such as Akai and Korg use have proprietary formats. Note that samplers can't always read all formats.

### Good samples

The digital quality of a sample or digital recording is expressed in bits and kHz (kilohertz). Higher figures indicate a better sample quality.

### Bit depth and sampling rate

A regular audio CD is 'sampled' at 16-bit/44.1 kHz.

- A lower **bit depth**, expressed in a number of bits, will make the sample less dynamic, which reduces differences between soft and loud and increases hiss.

- A lower **sampling rate** (expressed in kHz) will make for duller, poorer, and less natural sounding samples, but the file size will be smaller.

Many high-end instruments use 24-bit/96 kHz sampling.

### Sample editing

Sampling is more than just making a digital recording of a sound. It also involves editing. Samplers offer various editing options, such as *truncate* (cut off everything you don't need), *loop* (make a long sound based on a shorter sample), *normalize* (equalize the loudness of various samples), *reverse*, *slice* (cut them into pieces that can then be triggered separately), and so on.

# EFFECTS

All but some entry-level instruments have one or more effects to enhance your performance.

### Reverb

*Reverb*, the most common effect type, provides ambience, warmth, and spaciousness to the sound. Without reverb, amplified musical instruments tend to sound very 'dry.' Digital instruments usually offer a number of reverb types, most of which are named after the type of room they emulate: room, stage, auditorium, concert hall, or church, for example. Most digital reverbs also offer simulations of other types of reverbs such as the spring reverb that is use in many guitar amplifiers.

**TIP**

### Master effect

*Reverb is a master effect, meaning that it's commonly used on all or most instruments in the mix: accompaniment tracks, melody, and vocals.*

### Chorus

*Chorus* is another popular effect. The added fullness, presence, character, and spaciousness of a chorus work great for electric pianos, strings, guitar accompaniments, and pad sounds (see page 95). Many instruments provide various types of chorus, up to twenty or more.

### Digital signal processor

The effects in digital instruments are generated and controlled by one or more *digital signal processors* (*DSP*). If an instrument has just one DSP, you can commonly use just one effect at the time. With two DSPs, you're a lot more flexible: You can use reverb over the entire mix and add a little chorus on your electric piano sound, for example.

### More DSPs

Higher-level instruments often have one DSP for reverb effects, one for chorus effects, and one or more for other effects. Keyboards with a microphone input often have a dedicated DSP for vocal effects.

### Number of effects

**78**

The number of effects may vary from one to a hundred or more, with various types of each effect, effect combinations, and with both preset and user-definable effects.

## Effects

Chorus and reverb are just two of the many effects you can come across. Here are some of the others:

- **Flangers and phasers** offer two variations on the chorus effect. A phaser makes for a sweeping or swirling effect, and flanging adds anything between a departing jet plane and a slight, metallic, sweeping edge to the sound. Flangers, phasers, and choruses are the best-known *modulation effects*.

- **A delay or echo** repeats the note you've just played. A very short delay (up to around 40 ms) repeats the note a split second after you played it, making the sound a little fatter (*doubling*). Long delay times allow you to play along with the echoed notes.

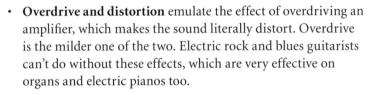

### Ambient effects

*Delay, echo, and reverb are known as* ambient effects.

- **Overdrive and distortion** emulate the effect of overdriving an amplifier, which makes the sound literally distort. Overdrive is the milder one of the two. Electric rock and blues guitarists can't do without these effects, which are very effective on organs and electric pianos too.

- An **enhancer** makes for a brighter, tighter, more sparkling, and cleaner sound with additional presence and detail.

- **Tremolo** rhythmically varies the sound's volume (*amplitude modulation*). Works well on some electric piano sounds.

- **Rotor or rotary** are two of the many terms that indicate an digital emulation of a Leslie speaker cabinet (see page 155), which literally swirls the sound around. This effect can usually be set at two speeds, *chorale* (slow) and *tremolo* (high).

- **Ping-pong** sends the first note to the right speaker, the following note to the left speaker, and so on.

79

*Setting the speed of a rotary effect.*

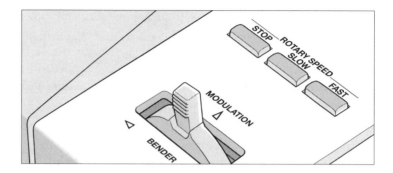

- **Panning, panorama, or pan** is a control you also find on mixing boards, allowing you to position an instrument in the stereo mix anywhere from far left to far right. *Auto pan* makes the sound smoothly move from left to right.

- A **wah-wah** does exactly what its name sounds like. With an *auto-wah*, the effect level is controlled by how loud you play.

- A **ring modulator** turns your music into unpredictable weird, clanking, bell-like sounds. Commonly used on organs and electric pianos.

- **Lo-fi**, the opposite of hi-fi, makes the instrument sound as if it's played through a vintage, beaten-up portable radio.

- **A compressor** reduces dynamic differences, boosting soft notes and reducing the level of loud notes. Electric guitarists use a compressor to make their notes sustain.

- **EQ** (see page 65) is usually considered an effect too.

**TIPCODE**

*Tipcode KEYS-010*
*Digital pianos and keyboards feature various on-board effects, such as reverb, chorus, wah-wah, flanger, and delay. Listen to some examples of what these effects can do.*

## Harmony

*Harmony* or *auto harmonize* are two of the many names for an effect that creates *harmonies* by adding one or more extra notes to the notes that you play, so you hear two, three, or even more pitches instead of one. The chords that you play are taken into account, preventing inappropriate notes: If you play a C-minor chord with your left hand, the effect will add an E♭ rather than an E to your solo part.

## Harmony types

Even entry-level instruments sometimes offer several types of harmony to choose from. One will add a note an octave above the note you're playing; another will add a third (major or minor, depending on the type of chord you're playing) or a fifth above, or the third and fifth step of a chord, sounding either above or below the note you're playing, and so on. Some of these harmony types fit a certain style of music (e.g., big band or country); others are meant to enhance certain sounds, such as string ensembles.

**Tipcode KEYS-011**
*The harmony feature adds your selection of notes to the notes you're playing, as demonstrated in this Tipcode.*

TIPCODE

## Arpeggiator

An *arpeggiator* is another effect that helps create the impression that you're doing more than you really are. When you play a chord, an arpeggiator makes it sound as though you're playing the notes involved — and a number of related notes — in a (usually) fast, repetitive sequence: It breaks up your chords in single notes. Every arpeggiator offers a choice of different patterns. Arpeggiators are a common feature on synths and workstations, but you may find them on some keyboards too.

81

**Tipcode KEYS-012**
This Tipcode briefly demonstrates an arpeggiator at work.

### Tweaking effects

You can often tweak any of the built-in effects to your liking. The more elements you can adjust and the more precisely you can adjust them, the more musical use the effects will generally have.

### Depth, rate, level

One clear example would be a chorus, which may have two or more parameters. The effect's *depth* sets the depth of the chorus effect. With *rate* you control the tempo of the effect. *Mix level* adjusts how much of the chorus effect you hear and how much of the original, clean sound.

**Tipcode KEYS-013**
Here's is a short demonstration of what you can do with the parameters of the chorus effect, adjusting depth and speed.

### Vibrato

Vibrato has similar parameters: the depth and speed of the pitch variation, and the *delay time* (how long it lasts before vibrato sets in). On less sophisticated instruments, you may be able to set only the intensity of an effect (e.g., light, normal and deep), or not even that.

### Considerations

Here are some additional points to consider when looking at effects sections:

- If you can control effect settings in **real time**, you can adjust things on the spot rather than being required to go through a couple of menus to adjust your delay, for example.

- It makes things much more musical if you can **adjust the tempo** (rate) of a delay or a tremolo to the tempo of the song, preferably with a tap tempo control: You simply tap the desired tempo, and the effect follows.

- It's also good to be able to **independently adjust the levels** of the selected effects for the various voices in layered sounds, for example.

- If you don't want to remember and recreate your effect settings every time you play, you need an instrument with **user presets**, which allow you to store and recall things.

- On some instruments, you can make **effect combinations**. If you connect two effects *in series*, the first effect will be processed by the second. Possible combinations are overdrive and flanger or delay; distortion and chorus, flanger, or delay; or chorus and delay. If you connecting effects *in parallel* (chorus and flanger, for example), the two effects do not influence each other.

### Judging effects

To properly judge effects, you need to know how to use them. Using effects is like using spices when cooking: Adding a bit of flanging can work great, but overdoing it may ruin the sound. And chorus is great for electric piano voices, but it makes acoustic pianos sound terribly out of tune — which, in certain situations, may be exactly what you want to do. Note that the quality and character of the available effects varies per brand and per instrument: Digital distortions can sound just right (warm and fat), or way too edgy or harsh; reverbs can be clean and crisp, or so muddy and soggy that you lose detail, and so on.

83

### Tipbook

If you want to learn more about effects and how to use them, and about using additional effect devices, check out *Tipbook Amplifiers and Effects* (see page 220).

# VOCAL PROCESSORS

Instruments with a microphone input often have a separate vocal processor, which features various effects dedicated to vocal performance.

### Harmonies

You can usually add harmonies to your voice, so you can create a virtual chorus or add backing vocals to your songs. Depending on the specifications of the instrument, you may be able to make your solo voice sound like a trio or a quartet; a male choir, a female choir, or a children choir; close-harmony or Andrew Sisters-style.

### Some other features

- A **gender function** or *voice transformer* can make a male voice sound female, or vice versa. Likewise, you can make your voice sound like a baby, a rapper, or an alien.

- A **vocoder** makes your voice sound synthetic or robot-like.

- A few instruments feature auto-tune, a device that automatically tunes the notes you sing to the correct pitch.

- A more common feature is a button that switches the vocal processor **off**, so you can address your audience in-between songs without the effects you use for singing.

- A **vocal remover**, *vocal canceller*, or *voice killer* removes the solo singing voice of prerecorded songs, so you can sing along yourself.

### Karaoke

That said, some keyboards can double as karaoke machines,

showing the lyrics on the display or an external monitor (see page 57). Karaoke song files are available online.

# SYNTHESIS OPTIONS

Keyboards with one or more synthesis options let you alter or edit your sounds, though usually less extensively than dedicated synthesizers will. You can give sounds a smoother or sharper attacks or rounder or more angular 'shapes'; change their timbre through time, or play them backwards, etc.

### Envelope generator
An *envelope generator* sets the 'contour' of a sound. The four parameters of an envelope generator are attack, decay, sustain, and release (ADSR).

* **Attack** is the time a sound takes to reach its maximum volume level.

* **Decay** is the time it takes the sound to drop to its sustain level, i.e., the level at which a sound continues while holding the key down.

* **Release** is how long the sound continues after releasing the key.

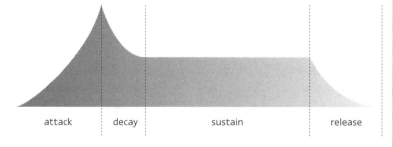

attack    decay       sustain       release

### Filters
A few keyboards have filters that you can use to let certain frequencies pass, while cutting off others. This allows you to alter sounds dramatically.

**85**

*TIPCODE*

**Tipcode KEYS-014**
*Here are some samples of what you can do with ADSR: Short release; long decay and long sustain; short decay and long sustain; slow attack and long release.*

- A **low pass filter** cuts off the frequencies above a specific point (this *cut-off frequency* may be adjustable);

- A **high pass filter** cuts off the frequencies below a certain point (same here);

- A **band pass filter** lets you control the frequencies that can pass the filter unaffected, while cutting off other frequencies.

'Real' synthesizers usually provide you with different, very flexible filter types.

### Low frequency oscillator (LFO)

An *LFO* (*low frequency oscillator*) is an electronic device that produces a slow (low-frequency) 'wave' that can be used to rhythmically influence the volume (i.e., tremolo), pitch (vibrato), or timbre (wah-wah) of a sound. On a few keyboards, you can set

**Tipcode KEYS-015**
*The effect of low and high pass filters is briefly demonstrated in this Tipcode.*

**86**

the intensity, rate, and delay of the LFO. Real synthesizers offer a lot more options, such as the choice of different waveforms, each of which has a different effect on the sound. If you would use an LFO to vary your volume level, a *square wave* would mean the volume is continuously switched on and off abruptly, while a *sawtooth wave* would make it go up gradually and go down quickly, just like the shape of a sawtooth suggests.

# OLD AND NEW MEDIA

With the arrival of USB ports and media cards, the old floppy disk drive has become (almost) obsolete. That's a good thing, because floppy disks were not very reliable, and slow. Still, many home keyboards featured a floppy disk drive (FDD) long after these disks had become obsolete for computer users.

### Hard disk
A hard disk allows you to access data much faster, and hard disks can store lots of data, including WAV files. Hard disks are less road-tough than media cards or data cards, which have no moving parts.

### Other storage media
Most other storage media that are introduced for computer, find their way into musical instruments as well, from USB sticks to SmartMedia cards and CompactFlash cards, SD cards, and other universal data cards. These cards are road-tough (no moving parts) and small (some no larger than a postage stamp). They also provide quick access to their data, so you can use them in real time. Their capacity varies from a couple of megabytes to several gigabytes, and more in the future. Note that some instruments can't handle higher capacity data cards.

### CD burner
A few instruments still feature an integrated CD burner that lets you store audio files (WAV) and MP3 files, and back up your own

87

*SmartMedia card.*

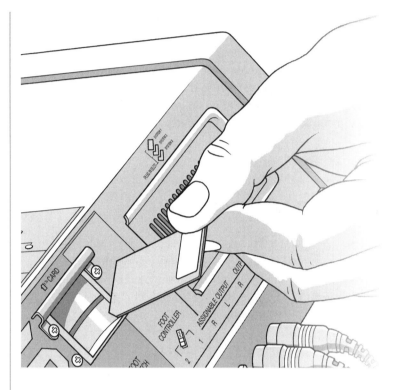

styles, registrations, sounds, and so on. As an alternative, you may just as well connect your instrument to your computer and its built-in CD burner instead.

### MP3 player

Other keyboards come with a built-in MP3 player, which may allow you to transpose songs, change the tempo of a song in real time, or record your own MP3 songs.

### USB recorder

Another option that you might like is a USB Audio Recorder: Plug

**TIP**

### Songs

*On a 4GB memory card, you can typically store some three to four hundred MP3 songs.*

**88**

in your USB stick and make an audio recording of your music, including vocals.

# JUST LIKE COMPUTERS

Despite their general appearance, most electronic musical instruments are essentially computers that produce sound.

### Operating system

Just like computers, these instruments have an operating system (OS). Most companies provide online updates. Just like new software for your computer, an update may bring you new functions and features, or just a better, bug-free instrument. These updates are usually free of charge.

### New sounds and songs

Likewise, many companies offer new sounds, songs, drum sets, and styles online. Download them directly into your instrument, or copy them to a USB stick and use this stick for your data transfer. Some instruments have their own LAN connector. Simply connect such an instrument to the Internet and it will automatically take you to the company's portal where you can download songs, styles, and so on.

TIP

### *Hardware expansion*

*Synthesizers and workstations can often be expanded with new hardware — which, by the time you read this, may have become more widespread as an option for keyboards and digital pianos too. Companies market expansion boards that offer anything from sampling to extra sounds (wave expansion boards), a video interface (see page 57), an arpeggiator, extra synthesizer power with added polyphony or effect processors, various tone generators, and so on.*

89

# EDUCATIONAL FEATURES

Though they can't replace a real teacher, the educational features that some instruments offer can make it easier to get started, make practicing more effective, or help you expand your knowledge.

### One hand at a time
One very common way to use your keyboard as a practicing tool was already mentioned on page 28. You can play back the (pre-)recorded left or right hand part and then play along with your other hand, so you practice one hand at the time. Some instruments have a hundred or more pre-recorded songs available that can be played back one hand at a time.

### Tempo
It helps if you can set the tempo, so you can either record a piece slowly and play it back at the intended speed, or slow a recording down so you can play along. With a *phrase trainer*, you can select a section of the song and play it back (at the original tempo, or slower) until you master it.

### Modes
More advanced systems also offer other ways to learn pre-recorded songs, often providing various modes. An example.

- One mode lets you concentrate on your **timing** of the notes; no matter which key you play, it will always produce the right pitch (a*ny key play* or *timing mode*).

- A second mode is about playing **the correct melody note**; the left hand part or the accompaniment will wait until you have played it (*waiting mode*).

- The third mode requires you to play all notes **in time, using the right keys**.

At the end of the song, a computerized voice may tell you how well you did. The instrument may even grade your work to help you keep track of your progress.

### Which key?

Some instruments tell you which keys to play, either by indicating them on the display, or by using *lighted keys*: You simply play the keys that light up. Dual lighting systems use different colors for the left and right hand parts.

### On display

The correct fingering may be displayed too (1 is your thumb; 2 your index finger, etc.), or a digital voice may tell you which finger to use for the next note. Some keyboards count the beats out loud (*'One, two, three; One, two, three'*) or tell you the name of the note you're supposed to play (C, D, E, and so on).

### Chords

Additionally, an instrument may be able to help you figure out chords. Or you can play your pre-programmed chords by simply pressing any key in the lower section, so you can focus on the melody or your solo. Some instruments even offer guidance in advanced subjects like counterpoint and harmony.

> ### Standard teaching methods
>
> *Also available are pianos with educational software that can be used in conjunction with standard piano teaching methods.*

TIP

### Games

Musical keyboard games come in many variations: The instrument sounds a note or a chord, and you have to guess which one it was; it plays a rhythmical pattern, which you have to repeat; and so on.

# USER'S MANUAL

Keyboards and most digital pianos offer more than you may be

91

able to find out by yourself. Even for advanced players, a user's manual is usually indispensable.

### Cover to cover

Reading the manual from cover to cover is a lot of work, but it will tell you everything the instrument is capable of and where to find things for future reference. Unfortunately, manuals often have an incomplete index, making it hard to re-find specific information without having to go through the entire book again.

# 6

# Sound

*An instrument may have a thousand features — but first and foremost, you should like the way it sounds. This chapter deals with the various types of sounds, sound quality, methods for judging sounds, and amplification.*

If you use a digital piano to play classical or jazz piano music, you may be perfectly happy if it has just one good, dynamic piano sound. But if you want to be a one-man band, or use a keyboard to arrange music for a band or a larger group of musicians, you're better off with an instrument that provides you with a thousand-plus sounds to choose from.

### Budget and sound

More money usually buys you more sounds. Entry-level keyboards often have a hundred sounds or more, while mid- and pro-level instruments may offer over a thousand different voices. On digital pianos, the number of sounds usually varies between a handful on the least expensive models to forty or more on higher-level instruments. However, price differences don't reflect the number of sounds as much as their quality.

### Three basic categories

The sounds on a typical keyboard fall into three basic categories: samples of acoustic instruments, samples of 'artificial' synthesizer sounds, and samples of sound effects such as ringing phones and gunshots. The acoustic instruments are the largest group.

### Shamisen

The names of the 'acoustic' voices are usually self-explanatory, but a little knowledge makes it easier to choose the right sounds for your performance: You may never consider using the subtle sound of a shamisen in a song if you have no idea what a shamisen actually is. Or you may do a lot of work to layer the voices of two violins, a viola, and a cello, simply because you didn't know that you have a built-in 'string quartet' that produces exactly that combination of sounds.

### Synthesizer and pad sounds

Keyboards also provide a selection of synthesizer sounds, using more or less descriptive names such as techno, saw lead, funky lead, adrenaline, and attack saw. *Pad sounds* are synthetic, dream-like, fantasy sounds with a very slow attack, sporting names like space voice, halo pad, fantasia, or dark moon.

**Tipcode KEYS-016**
*Typical pad and synthesizer sounds can be found on any home keyboard. Here are two examples.*

### Style-related sounds
Some instruments also have groups of sounds for certain musical styles, such as techno or R&B, or they have special DJ sounds on board.

### Drum sets
Keyboards and ensemble pianos offer various types of drum sets to meet your needs: A heavy metal act requires a different type of drum sound than a jazz tune or a rap song. Keyboards usually have a choice of standard drum sets ('regular' sounding drums), one or more brush sets for jazz ballads, Cuban and Latin sets with congas, bongos, and other hand percussion instruments, electronic or synth sets for dance music, and so on. Some also feature symphonic percussion (timpani, symphonic cymbals, concert toms, etc.), African sets (such as talking drums, djembe, or bougarabou), or other ethnic percussion sets.

### Manual drums
Most keyboards can be used as a drum machine too: If you hit a button labeled *drums* or *m(anual) drums*, or if you select the 'drums' voice, you can play the instrument's drum and percussion sounds with the keys. When choosing an instrument, compare the drum sounds of various models and brands carefully to which set would work best for your music.

### Special attention
Pay special attention to the bass drum and snare drum sounds (you're bound to use these drums more than others) and to the

95

cymbal sounds. The latter are extremely hard to catch in samples. The various percussion instruments are usually triggered by the same keys on different instruments: The bass drum on key C3, the snare drum on E3, and the closed hi-hats on F♯3, for example.

*On many keyboards, small icons tell you which keys trigger which percussion instruments.*

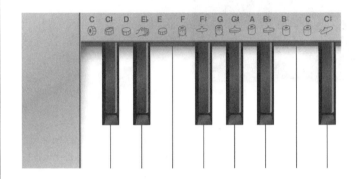

### Two samples
Some instruments have different samples under one key: a regular timbale sound when played not too loud, and a timbale rimshot when you hit the same key harder, for example.

## GOOD SOUNDS

Judging sounds is mainly a matter of taste: You may like one piano sound better than the other, of course, even though the other has better technical specifications. Still, some knowledge on how sound quality is determined can make it easier to find the instrument you like best.

### Not like you
If you play higher and lower notes on an acoustic instrument, it isn't only the pitch that changes. The sound gets a different timbre too. If you record a note played on a piano, and play it back at double the speed, it will sound an octave higher — but it doesn't sound much like a piano anymore. Likewise, if you record yourself singing a note and you play it back an octave higher, it doesn't

sound like you anymore. So for a sampled instrument to sound realistic at various pitches, its acoustic counterpart needs to have been sampled at various pitches.

**Tipcode KEYS-017**
Playing a recorded note at twice the speed sounds way different from playing or singing a note that sounds an octave higher.

TIPCODE

### One or more per octave
On very low cost instruments, there may be no more than a single sample per octave: With a five-octave keyboard, that would add up to five grand piano samples, five tenor saxophone samples, and so on. However, to make a voice sound anything like the real thing, one sample per key is the minimum.

### More per key
To have a sampled instrument sound even more natural, you need various samples per key. Why? Because playing an instrument louder also changes the timbre of the sound. It gets brighter, usually, and the attack may get more aggressive, and there will be more sustain.

### Filters or samples
This effect can be imitated, to a certain extent, by using filters that lets more high frequencies pass as you play louder. This makes for a more natural sound, but it's still not as good as playing and recording each note at various volume levels. On high-quality instruments, there may be three, four, or more samples per note.

### From one to the next
When you play increasingly louder, the instrument should go from

97

one sample to the next without you hearing that it does. Various techniques (e.g., *velocity crossfade* and *physical modeling*; see page 99) are used to make this a smooth process, just like it is with an acoustical instrument.

### Rates
The bit depth and sampling rate of the samples (see page 77) tell you a bit about their quality, but these figure are usually not provided with the instrument.

> ### Stereo
> *Stereo samples will make a digital piano sound natural by adding depth and dimension to the sound. A stereo sample takes up twice the amount of memory of a mono sample!*

### Long samples
The long sustaining sound of a low piano note requires a very long sample. It is cheaper to use a shorter sample and loop the sound, slowly decreasing the volume level. Looped samples usually don't sound as natural. Listen closely and see if you can tell.

### Memory
All the above features (more samples per key, stereo samples, long samples) require additional sample memory. Some figures for your reference: Sample memory, often indicated as *Wave ROM*, may vary from 8MB on a low budget keyboard to 64 or 128MB on midrange instruments and 256MB on the most expensive models.

### Piano samples
That's not a whole lot, actually. While grand piano samples may take up less than a megabyte on entry-level instruments and more than 80MB on a high-quality digital piano, there are piano samples of more than 5GB as well. It speaks for itself that these differences can be heard.

### Sound improvement
There are many more ways to improve sound quality on a digital

98

instrument. Adding a bit of vibrato, for example, or including some of the mechanical sounds that acoustic instruments make, like fret sounds or squeaking strings on guitars. Some companies use a lot of reverb to hide the lower quality of their samples. These instruments may sound impressive at first, but they tend to get tiresome after a while.

### Technology
Physical modeling offers another means to enhance these sounds. This involves using computer models to emulate characteristics of acoustic instruments, such as the sizes and weights of hammers in a grand piano, the mass of the tone bar or the location of the pickup in an electric piano, the resonance of the piano strings when the damper pedal is used (*sympathetic resonance*: the undamped strings resonating along with the notes being played), the residual resonance of the   soundboard, and so on.

### Tone wheel organ
Other popular sampled sounds may reflect just as much attention to details as the piano samples. For example, samples of tone wheel organs (see pages 154–155) may simulate the 'leakage' noise that comes from the tone wheels, or the click sound generated by older tone wheel organs whose contacts need cleaning.

# AUDITIONING INSTRUMENTS

Judging the sounds of musical instruments is mainly a matter of comparing them. It's hard easy — if not impossible — to truly remember the timbre of a specific instrument, so this is best done in one session. Remember, however, that your ears will need a break before you think they do. So take five, now and then.

### One at a time
If you want to make choice between two or more keyboards or pianos, always remember to compare no more than one type of sound at a time. Focus on the types of sounds you're likely to use most. So for example, first select the best piano sound on each

99

instrument and compare those piano voices. Then do the same with the organs, various string sounds, and so on.

### Choose the right instruments

Some instruments have great electric guitar sounds but average acoustic guitar voices. Others have great organs but disappointing saxophones. You can ask a sales person to offer recommendations based on the sounds you're commonly using.

> ### Jazz or classical
> It's good to know which type of sound fits the music you play. If you play classical piano music only, you'll need a piano sound that offers plenty of dynamics and nuance; a piano in a rock band should sound a lot brighter, with more attack, while dynamics are typically less important.

### An expensive one

Even if you're looking for a low-budget or mid-price instrument, it may be good to include some really expensive ones in your search: Their sounds will help you set a standard that you can aim for.

### Acoustic piano

Likewise, if you plan to buy a portable keyboard, it's good to listen to the piano or grand piano voices of some digital pianos too. You can also listen to some acoustic pianos first, so you get an idea of what they really sound like.

### How to play it

Even the very best sample of a saxophone or an violin won't *sound* anywhere near the real thing if you don't *play* it as you would play the real thing. In other words: You shouldn't play typical keyboard licks using a saxophone or guitar sound, for example. To emulate the sound of an instrument, you need to translate onto the keyboard the way that instrument is played: Different instruments require completely different keyboard technique. Likewise, you should judge sounds in their proper context. Have the keyboard

**100**

play a rock accompaniment when you audition rock guitar sounds, for example.

> ### The real thing
> Keyboard makers continuously try to allow their products to make 'real' instruments come to life. Most innovations are introduced on their high-end keyboards. Some examples include adding the finger noise of changing positions on the guitar neck, or the sound of a pick on the strings, or the possibility to use six keys to 'pluck' the virtual strings of a guitar (where the pitches of these keys change according to the chord you're playing with your left hand), or to emulate different strumming techniques, both in real time.

### Harpsichords and Clavinets
It also helps to know a bit about the character of the 'instruments' you are judging. A harpsichord is supposed to sound very classical (and lack dynamics!), while the vaguely related Clavinet is usually supposed to sound extremely funky, for example.

### The range
Try the main sounds throughout their range. Most sounds do very well in the middle of the keyboard, but do they get too harsh or too thin in the high range, or too muddy or indistinct in the low range? On lower quality instruments, voices sometimes sound acceptable within a relatively small range only.

### The natural range
Remember that 'real' instruments have limited ranges. You can't expect a bass sample to still sound like a bass if you play it at a higher pitch than the real instrument can sound, and you can't expect choir samples to sound like anything human if you play them at the extreme ends of the keyboard.

### Words
Musicians often use very subjective words to describe what they're

101

hearing. What one finds shrill (and thus unattractive), another may describe as bright (and thus attractive). Still, using such words can make it easier to find what you're looking for. It's more effective if you know that you're looking for a transparent, colorful sound with bright highs and strong mids, rather than just a 'great' sound.

### Miscellaneous tips

• Listen to **how sensitive** the sounds are to variations in touch. Classical pianists should pay special attention to the pedals too (see pages 48–49).

• When comparing specific voices on various instruments, make sure to set their **volumes to equal levels**.

• Compare sounds **without using effects** — and compare effects separately.

• Organs, synth sounds, flutes, and drum sounds are relatively **easy to sample**, so they will usually sound good. Pianos, guitars, saxes and cymbals are a lot harder to get right.

• **String sections** often sound more convincing than individual string instruments, such as violin and cello.

### Headphones

Decent quality headphones, available for less than fifty dollars, usually sound a lot better than the built-in speakers. If you intend to use external amplification, auditioning the instrument via phones will give you a more honest impression of how good the sounds and effects really are. As headphones exclude the performance of the onboard speakers and amplification, they can also help in comparing samples on various instruments. Tip: Always play your headphones at a moderate volume level to prevent hearing damage.

### The lowest notes

When you're auditioning instruments using their built-in speakers, you might not be able to get the lowest notes to sound as loud and strong as the high ones. With their limited dimensions (and often enough, their low cost), the instrument's speakers are often unable to truly reproduce these low frequencies. If possible, hook the instrument up to an external sound system. The response is supposed to be even at all pitches, low to high.

### The difference
If you have three saxophonists play the same saxophone, you'll hear three different timbres. Have one player play the instrument while using different mouthpieces and different reeds, and you'll hear a different timbre every time. Have the same player play a ballad on it, then a funky riff, and finally a classical phrase, and you'll hear three distinctly different voices coming from the same instrument and the same player — and so on. No matter how many features they have, digital instruments will probably never be that expressive. They do, however, offer possibilities that acoustic players can only dream of.

# AMPLIFICATION: THE SPEAKERS

Any keyboard instrument's sound has a lot to do with the quality of its built-in amplifier and speakers. Two remarks in advance:

- Many keyboard makers use **the exact same samples** for instruments in various price ranges. If so, the more expensive ones sound better simply because they have a better sound system.

- All keyboards and many digital pianos will benefit from an **external sound system**. If you plan take the instrument on the road, you can't do without one.

### Size
When it comes to speakers, size isn't everything. Some small ones are good, some large ones aren't.

### Two or more
Most basic instruments have two speakers; one left, one right. More advanced models have separate speakers or *drivers* for

103

the low range (*woofer*), and the mid-high ranges. This usually provides you with punchier basses, more pronounced mid-range frequencies, and brighter highs. In concentric speakers, the mid- or high-range driver is centered in the woofer, which can make the unit look as if it's only one speaker (i.e., *concentric speakers* or *dual cone speakers*). Tip: The fact that an instrument has two speakers or two sets of speakers doesn't mean that all its sounds are stereo samples.

### Four or more
Digital pianos — especially grand models — often have four or even more speakers to approximate the spatial characteristics of the acoustic instrument. A six-speaker three-way system consists of two sets (stereo) of three (low, mid, high) speakers.

### Speaker location
Keyboard speakers are usually mounted in the front panel, facing you directly. On most digital pianos, it's hard to find them. Some pianos have separate *tweeters*, which produce the high frequencies, mounted above the keyboard, aiming the sound more toward your ears. A few instruments come with adjustable speakers.

TIP

> ### Lows
> *In many styles of dance music, predominant lows are extremely important. That's why many keyboard speakers have bass-enhancing ports, and some even come with an (optional) subwoofer.*

### Hi-fi
The best way to judge speakers is to listen to them much as you would listen to a pair of hi-fi speakers. How's the balance between low end, midrange, and treble? Can they handle strong bass sounds and electric guitar stabs without distorting? Do you still hear a full, dynamic sound at low volume levels?

# AMPLIFICATION: THE AMP

Good digital pianos usually have more powerful amplifiers than keyboards. The extra power is not meant to make the instrument sound louder, but to faithfully reproduce the dynamic range of an acoustic piano.

### Figures
The power output of the stereo amplifiers in keyboards and low-budget digital pianos is usually somewhere between 2x5 and 2x15 watts. More expensive pianos have more powerful amps, with power ratings from some 30 to 100 or more watts per channel.

### Bi-amping
Some instruments have separate, powerful amps for the low frequencies, as true bass reproduction requires a lot of power. For example, a piano may have a 2x70 watt amplifier for the low frequencies and a 2x30 watt amp for the mid and high range. This is known as *bi-amping*. Please note that there are companies that advertise such a combination as a '200 watt sound system' by simply adding up all those figures, but this is not how it works.

### 3D
To make instruments sound more spacious, they may feature *3D stereo enhancers*, *wide stereo controls*, and so on. Some can even be hooked up to a home theatre system for a surround sound playing experience.

# EXTERNAL AMPLIFICATION

An external sound system will substantially improve the performance of most instruments. This should be no surprise, since a dedicated amplifier/speaker combination easily costs as much as an mid-price keyboard. The solutions offered in this chapter also work for speaker-less stage pianos. If you want to know more about amplification, speakers, mixers, and so on, check out *Tipbook Amplifiers and Effects* (see page 220).

### Home stereo

You may try to improve the sound of your instrument by using your home stereo system instead of the built-in sound system. Do this only if you're sure that your stereo system can handle a keyboard instrument. Read the appropriate manuals first, as well as page 122 of this book. Remember that you should *never* connect your keyboard instrument to the phono or disc input of your home sound system, as this input is designed to handle only the very weak signals from a record player. Instead, use one of the inputs marked *tape in*, *CD*, *aux*, or *tuner*.

### Keyboard amps

Your instrument will sound a lot better if you use one or two dedicated keyboard amplifiers. They're usually *combo amps*, with both the actual amplifier and the speakers in a single cabinet. Most keyboard amps have a 10", 12", or 15" woofer, and a separate tweeter or horn for the high frequency ranges.

*A very basic keyboard amp.*

106

## Two

For small venues, a 60 to 100 watt keyboard combo with a 12"
woofer will usually suffice. Such amps start at around two
hundred fifty dollars. Note that you will probably want to buy two
of them. After all, a single amp will not give you the stereo sound
that your instrument is capable of; stereo will enhance most effects

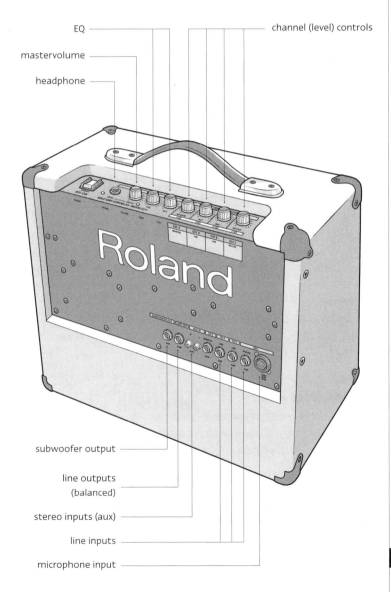

EQ — channel (level) controls

mastervolume

headphone

*A keyboard amp with extra inputs. (Roland)*

subwoofer output

line outputs (balanced)

stereo inputs (aux)

line inputs

microphone input

107

as well as your overall sound. There are not many keyboard amps that supply more than some 150 watts of power. For larger venues, most keyboardists use a PA system to amplify their instrument.

### Mini-PA

Keyboard amps often have extra inputs for other instruments and/ or microphones, a built-in equalizer (see page 66), effect connectors, and one or more extra outputs. This allows you to use them as miniature PA systems or as stage monitors. Price differences in amps with identical power ratings are usually due to the overall quality, the quality of the built-in speakers, and the available features.

### Powered monitors

You can also create your own portable PA system by purchasing a set of powered monitors and a small mixer. Complete systems are also available. Basically, a powered monitor is a box that houses one or more speakers and a one or two power amps, the latter providing separate amplification of the bass and treble frequency ranges (bi-amping; see page 105). The mixer houses the preamp and allows you to control volume levels, tone, and more. As an alternative, there are passive speakers (no amps built in) and powered mixers, which house both the power amp and the preamp.

### At home

If you play your instrument at home and want to improve the sound, you may consider buying a set of small *nearfield monitors*,

### Speakers off

When using an external sound system, you may still hear the instrument's onboard speakers. If you can't turn them off, or turn them down without reducing the overall output to zero, then plug your headphones in. It's even better to insert just the adapter plug that usually comes with it, as this prevents sound from leaking through the headphones. Some instruments have separate level controls for speakers and audio outs.

108

designed to be listened to from nearby. Such monitors often sound a lot better than your built-in instrument speakers, especially on home keyboards.

# 7

# Accompaniments

Just like a real band, the virtual band in a keyboard is
supposed to make you — the soloist — sound good. This
chapter introduces you to some of the details of auto-
accompaniment sections, the way they sound, and their
features.

The number of available styles on serious keyboards and ensemble pianos can vary from about sixty to a few hundred. Some offer two variations on each style, others as many as four, which helps to keep things interesting. After all, it can become a drag to hear the same country band play the same country groove in every country song.

### More styles
The specified number of styles of an instrument is less important if you can edit them or create new ones yourself (see page 119), or if you can add new styles from online sources. The number of available styles is staggering; you can find pretty much everything you need, from the latest dance beats to traditional Chinese styles.

### Groups or families
Every keyboard manufacturer seems to have its own ideas on how to categorize styles. Hip-hop may be filed under 'contemporary' or 'dance,' for example, and big band under 'jazz' or 'swing.' Some companies use categories that contain the styles of a certain era (for example: fifties or sixties: rock, boogie, twist, and so on) or a geographic area (e.g., European: polka, waltz, march, and so on); others don't.

### 8 or 16
Two more categories that you may find on some instruments and not on others are *8-beat* and *16-beat*, referring to rock rhythms in which the drummer plays eighth or sixteenth notes respectively.

### Focus
Likewise, some companies or individual instruments focus on 'traditional' styles such as jazz, rock, and Latin, while others are clearly dance oriented, with a focus on contemporary styles. Some also provide you with a large number of ethnic styles, while other have Western styles only.

### Piano only
Many instruments have a number of *pianist styles* that replace the single notes you play with your left hand with an impressive piano accompaniment.

112

## Comparing

Accompaniment sections are best judged style by style, concentrating on the ones you're most likely to use. Always compare styles at identical tempos and volume levels. (Styles usually have an assigned start-up tempo. This may be recalled automatically as soon as you select the style, or you may have to recall it by simultaneously pressing the +/- tempo buttons, for example.)

## Musicians

Ideally, the various musical styles have been programmed by experts: Latin musicians for Latin rhythms, jazz musicians for jazz styles, rockers for rock styles. Though virtual bands will (probably) never be able to replace live bands, they can sound amazingly good. When comparing styles, listen to how natural or musical the band sounds. Some sound as mechanical as they are, while others really seem to groove or swing. As the styles need to please a large group of customers, they're often more or less 'middle of the road.'

## Sample grooves

A few instruments have additional sample grooves (audio recordings of guitar phrases, drum grooves, background vocals, etc.) onboard, which cannot be edited. They can be combined with the common pre-programmed sequences, however. This enhances the feeling of playing live, with a real band.

## Busy or relaxed

Some manufacturers go for very busy accompaniments, with a lot of drums and percussion, intricate bass lines, and complex chords, while others consistently prefer more sparse arrangements. Flashy accompaniments may sound impressive, but may eventually become annoying.

---

### *Bare accompaniments*

*A tip: Start off by listening to only the bare accompaniments, without playing any chords. Then when you do hit a chord, you'll be able to tell how everything fits in together.*

TIP

**113**

### One by one

If you want to get the full picture of an instrument, then zap
through the styles one by one. Don't forget to check out the ones
you're unfamiliar with. They may inspire you to play things you've
never even dreamt of.

# THE BAND

Most styles, just like real life, provide you with a drummer and a
bassist as a basic rhythm section. Next there will be one or more
harmony instruments (piano, organ, or guitar, for example).
On top of that you may hear strings, woodwinds, brass, or other
melody instruments, and some percussion to spice things up. But
how does this all actually work?

### Number of tracks

Accompaniments have several *tracks* or *parts*, with each track
dedicated to one or more 'members' or sections of the band.

### The foundation

Often there is a track each for the drummer and the bass player,
who lay down a foundation for the other musicians to build on.
Drummers in particular can radically influence the sound and feel
of a group, so make sure you like your drummer and the drum
sounds (see pages 95–96). Like drum sounds, bass sounds vary
from style to style. Some use an upright bass, others use an electric
bass guitar or a synthesized bass sound, for example.

### Acc1, acc2, acc3

The remaining tracks are dedicated to harmony and any
additional instruments. They're usually marked *acc1, acc2, acc3*,
and so on, *acc* being short for *accompaniment.*

### Three to eight

The number of available tracks generally varies from three to
eight. The more tracks you have, the more parts you can play

114

simultaneously, and the more flexible your band is: You can usually choose which ones you want to hear and which ones you don't, or you can start with just a drum groove, then add a bassist, then a pianist, a horn section, strings, a guitarist, backing vocalists, etc. Advanced systems also allow you to set the volume level of each part or track.

### Small and large

On some instruments, you can switch between small and large ensembles, or you have options for *drum* and *bass, combo,* or *big band*, for example. Also, you may be able to enhance the band's performance with a series of buttons that trigger a trumpet section, a steel drummer, a funky guitarist or another musician that follows the chords you play. The choice of instrumentalists under these buttons is usually determined by the style you have chosen, but you may be allowed to make alternative selections.

> ### Morphing
> Some instruments allow for extra variations by letting you blend or morph parts from various styles. Samba drums and an upright bass in a hip hop band? No problem.

### Lower

A button marked *lower* or *left orchestra* lets you add a voice to what you play with your left hand, so you can add strings to the band, or guitar chords, or any other sound.

### Variations

All these possibilities add up to the pre-programmed style variations that every keyboard offers.

## CHORD RECOGNITION

Keyboards and ensemble pianos have various chord recognition modes. Here's what they are and how they work.

**115**

### One finger

A popular function allows you to play chords with just a single finger. Some familiar names for this mode are *one-finger chords, single-finger chords,* or *intelligent chords.* In this mode, pressing a C key in the chord recognition area produces a C-major chord, sounding the notes C, E and G. To play a C-minor chord in this mode, sounding the notes C, E♭ and G, you need to press the C key and the white D key above it. Adding the next white key results in a C seven chord (C7), sounding the notes C, E, G and B♭.

### Keys are switches

In this one-finger mode, the keys act like switches rather than keys: A single 'switch' produces a major chord, two adjacent switches produce a minor chord, and so on. This saves you from having to learn the way chords are built up. Some instruments can even produce minor, seventh, and other chords that match the key signature of the piece by pressing single keys only. (For more information on chords, please check out *Tipbook Music on Paper*; see page 222.)

### Fingered

In the *fingered* or *fingered chords* mode, you trigger the accompaniment by playing all the notes that make up the chord you want to hear.

### Full keyboard

In a third mode (*piano style, whole key, full keyboard, full mode,* or *full range*), the entire keyboard is turned into a chord recognition area: The chords are deducted from the harmonies that you play, and you can play the melody or a solo simultaneously.

*Different
modes.*

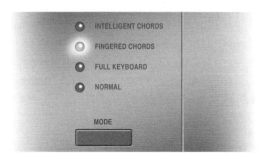

INTELLIGENT CHORDS

FINGERED CHORDS

FULL KEYBOARD

NORMAL

MODE

### Normal

In the *normal* mode, the accompaniment section is deactivated, and the instrument behaves like a regular piano, playing-wise. You may be able to keep a rhythmic backing going, but the rest of the band won't be around.

### Bass inversion

Virtual bassists usually play the root note of the chord. A function with names such as *bass inversion* or *fingered-on bass* allows you to have your bassist play other notes as well: If you play a C-major chord as C–E–G, the bassist will play the root (C). If you invert the chord and play it as E–G–C, for example, it's still a C-major chord, but the bass will sound an E (the lowest note of the inverted chord).

### G nine sharp eleven

There are many more chord types than the three mentioned above. All instruments will recognize the common chord types, and a growing number of accompaniment systems can also handle extended chords that include, for example, a ninth and a raised eleventh step (C9♯11: C–E–G–B♭–D–F♯).

# CONTROLLING THE BAND

Songs always consist of various sections linked to one another in sequence. They often start off with an intro, followed by a number of verses and choruses, and then finish off with an ending. Accompaniment sections help you emulate a real band by offering one or more automatic intros and endings, variations on the basic pattern that you can use for the choruses, and fills to link the sections to one another. More money usually buys you more options and more flexibility.

### Intros and endings

Playing an intro is usually a matter of providing the desired chord and hitting the intro button. To have the instrument provide a

**117**

*Accompani-
ment controls*

fully automatic ending, you simply hit the ending button. Better instruments offer a choice of (shorter, longer, and so on) intros and endings.

### Variations

You'll often use the basic pattern in a certain style for the verse of a song and select a variation for the chorus. These variations usually sound a bit busier than the basic pattern. The drummer may switch from timekeeping on the hi-hat to the ride cymbal, horns may be added, the feel or the rhythm may be changed, and so on.

### Synchro start and stop

When you use *synchro start*, the band won't kick in until you play a chord. This allows you to play an intro melody with your right hand. *Synchro stop* stops the band when you release the keys in the chord recognition area.

### Hold

The *hold* option, permanently switched on in most instruments, does the opposite of synchro stop: It keeps the band playing whether you are playing or not. Switching *hold* off, if the instrument has that option, will stop the chord and bass parts of the accompaniment as soon as you release the keys; only the drums keep playing.

### More than one

Advanced instruments offer a variety of endings, intros, variations, and fills or *breaks* per style. Some automatically play a fill when you go from one variation to the next, others only when you tell them to.

**118**

### Fade out, fade in

A *fade out* function allows you to gradually reduce the sound to silence rather than using an ending. *Fade in* does the opposite.

### Mix 'n' match

Fully-featured auto-accompaniments allow you to mix and match all kinds of options: fills with variations, synchro starts with intros, and so on.

### Groove control

Some keyboards feature *groove control*, slightly altering the exact timing of the band's notes to create a different, more 'human' rhythmic feel.

### Softer, please

You can usually adjust the balance between the accompaniment and the melody part you play, but you'll get a more musical performance if you can control the loudness of the band real time, by simply changing the volume at which you play the chords: When you play softer, the band follows — just like a real ensemble would, or at least should — and vice versa.

# DO-IT-YOURSELF

Sophisticated instruments often let you to create your own styles or edit existing ones by changing bass patterns, adding instruments, changing voices, editing effects, reducing the percussion section, or whatever you like.

### Save

You can always save the styles you've made or edited. You may able to save anywhere from eight up to 64 or more *user styles* or *RAM styles* next to the available, pre-programmed *ROM styles*. This is the maximum number of user styles that you can access directly; of course you can always save more styles on external storage media, such as a hard disk or a media card.

119

### *From scratch*

Programming a full accompaniment from scratch is not easy:
Every part and every section has to be composed and programmed
into the sequencer.

# 8

# Connections

*Headphones, amplifiers, additional instruments, mixers, you name it: Most keyboards and pianos come with a host of inputs and outputs for a host of possibilities.*

Pedal connectors (*control jacks*) have been covered in Chapter 5; MIDI connections are dealt with in Chapter 9. The other connections are explained in this chapter.

### First

Before you connect any cords to your instrument or any other electric or electronic devices, always read their manuals first. Also, turn all relevant volume controls down when connecting or disconnecting musical instruments, amplifiers, and other devices, and be sure that all devices have their power turned off.

### In and out

Connectors are also known as (*connection*) *terminals*, *sockets*, *receptacles*, or *jacks*. Some are inputs, which feed data or electric signals (i.e., power or audio signals) into the instrument. Other jacks are *outputs*, from where data or signals can be sent to other devices: mixers, speakers, an amplifier, or your computer, for example.

### Location

With the exception of the headphone jack(s), the connectors are usually located on the rear panel of the instrument. Some manufacturers identify these connectors on the front panel to make it easier to plug in or remove cables from corresponding positions in the back. A few instruments have their connectors on the left side panel.

*... identify the connections on the front panel...*

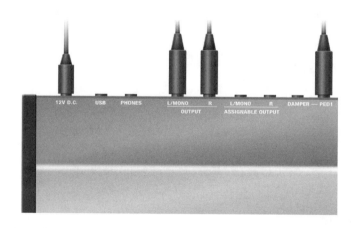

**122**

## Headphones

Most instruments have their headphone jack(s) below the keyboard, on the left-hand side. Having two headphone jacks is useful for lessons (one for you, one for your teacher), or if you want to play four-handed classical music on a digital piano, for example. Most headphone jacks are designed for 1/4" TRS phone plugs. TRS stands for tip, ring, and sleeve. Three wires can be attached to this plug (ground, left, and right), so it allows for the transmission of a stereo signal.

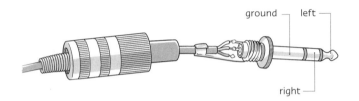

ground — left —

right —

*A TRS phone plug or jack plug.*

## Audio out

The audio outputs, labeled *line out*, *audio out*, or just *output*, are used to connect the instrument to an external sound system, a studio mixing console, or the line inputs of another instrument. There's usually one connector for the right channel and one for the left. One of them will be labeled mono, usually the left one (marked

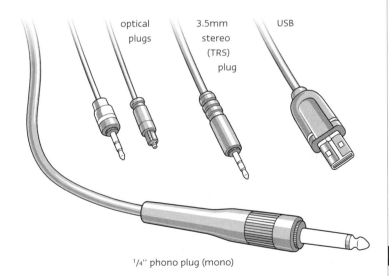

optical plugs

3.5mm stereo (TRS) plug

USB

*Various plugs.*

¹/₄'' phono plug (mono)

**123**

## Balanced outputs

Some high-end instruments have balanced outputs, using XLR connectors (see page 125) or TRS plugs. A balanced connection uses three wires, just like stereo connectors. The third wire, in this case, is used to cancel noise that might be picked up by the cable. Balanced connections are also known as symmetrical connections. There's much more on this subject in Tipbook Amplifiers and Effects (see page 220).

'L/MONO'). If you have a mono keyboard amp, use this socket. Audio outputs and inputs typically use large (¼") phone plugs.

### Prevent overload

If your instrument doesn't have separate audio outputs and you still want to use external amplification, you may try to use the headphone jack instead. Note that this output produces a pretty strong signal. Set the volume control on your instrument no higher than a quarter of the way, and then use the amp's volume control as the master control. This will usually prevent overload and possible damage to the amp and speakers. Remember that a dedicated audio output is better suited to the task of driving an external amplifier, so if your instrument has one, use it.

### Assignable outputs

Assignable outputs — very rare on the instruments covered in this book — let you send a particular track or a part of your performance to an external device. An example would be to use an external reverb, a distortion, or another effect on a certain part.

### Multimedia speakers

Speaker-less stage pianos sometimes have a stereo mini-jack that you can use for a pair of multimedia monitor speakers, allowing you to practice at low volumes.

### Line in

The *line* or *audio in* connectors can be used to connect another

124

instrument (so it uses the same amp and speakers as your instrument), or a CD player, an MP3 player, or another sound source, so that you can play along with pre-recorded music. Line inputs can also be used for sampling. Similar to the audio outputs, you need to use the one marked 'mono' if you want to connect a mono device.

*Various connections.*

## Effects
The line input is usually not routed through the internal effects. If you connect another instrument to this input, its sound will not be affected by the effects section of the main instrument.

## Gain control
Because different devices generate different output levels, it is helpful if the inputs have an adjustable *gain control* or *trim control*. This allows you to adjust the sensitivity of the input to match the connected equipment. Some inputs can handle anything from another electronic instrument or a CD-player (high output) to an electric guitar (relatively low output) or a microphone (very low output).

### XLR inputs
*Professional microphones use three-pin XLR connectors. The microphone is plugged into the female connector of the cable; the male connector plugs into the amplifier, or — in this case — into the microphone input of your keyboard. As said before, the balanced connection provided by using XLR reduces hum and noise. Another tip: Most condenser microphones use phantom power. They're powered 'invisibly' through the microphone cable. If a keyboard has an XLR input, check if it provides phantom power too!*

**125**

### Microphones

If your instrument has a dedicated microphone input, it will usually also have dedicated vocal effects (see page 84) that affect the signal from this input only. Of course, you can also use the microphone input for an acoustic guitar or the sound of any other acoustic instrument. A level control is usually provided. Check the manual to see which type of microphone is recommended, and check to see if your keyboard has an XLR microphone input.

### Send and return

A few instruments have special inputs and outputs to connect an external effect device. They are usually labeled send or auxiliary output and loop return or auxiliary input respectively. The output transmits the signal to the effect; the loop return receives the processed signal.

### Digital in/out

Digital inputs and outputs (AES/EBU or S/PDIF) are occasionally found on keyboards and digital pianos. Digital outputs are commonly used in studios only, while instruments with built-in samplers can benefit from a digital input for digital sound sources. Optical connectors use light to transmit data.

### Video out

A *video output* allows you to connect an additional display to show karaoke style lyrics to your audience, or display a slide show or even video to enhance your performance.

## COMPUTER CONNECTIONS

You can connect your instrument to your computer using MIDI (see Chapter 9) or a USB port, and some instruments (still) have an alternative connector.

### To host

A direct computer connection, usually a round connector marked to host or simply computer, allows you to use your computer for a variety of purposes, from recording and playing back your performances to saving or loading sounds, styles, and other data, or editing and printing the songs you play, and so on.

### USB ports

On most instruments, the connector mentioned above has been replaced by a (square, type B) USB port. If you use this port, your computer will recognize your instrument as an additional hard disk, allowing you to exchange data with the familiar drag and drop technique. You can also make audio recordings of your performances and store them on your computer's hard disk, burn them onto CD-Rs, or convert them into smaller MP3 files and send them to friends online, and so on.

### Storage

A flat USB port (type A) allows you to use a USB memory stick, for example, to load new songs, sounds, or styles into you instrument. If you still have lots of sounds, styles, or performances stored on floppy disks, you can also use this port to connect an external USB floppy disk drive. Tip: Some instruments have a second USB port on the front panel, providing easy access for your USB stick or plug.

### USB and MIDI

On some instruments, USB ports are used for MIDI too (see page 134).

### PC keyboard

A few instruments have an input for a computer keyboard, which you can use to enter lyric data into songs, or to give names to sounds, styles, or songs.

# 9

# MIDI

*Layering sounds is a great way to expand your creative possibilities. It's even better if you can layer the sounds of different instruments: Play one keyboard and have a voice of another keyboard or a synthesizer sound along. This is just one of the many possibilities offered by MIDI. This chapter gives you the basics.*

MIDI is a system that allows electronic musical instruments to communicate with each other. The four letters stand for *Musical Instrument Digital Interface*: It allows a digital connection (interface) between musical instruments. Traditionally, MIDI uses the five-pin connectors shown below. Modern instruments also use USB ports for MIDI (see page 134).

(see page 134)

*The in and out ports of the built-in MIDI interface.*

### Piano and strings

Suppose you have a digital piano and a portable keyboard, and you want to combine the grand piano voice of the piano with the keyboard's strings. You'll need to make the two instruments communicate with each other. How? You simply connect the MIDI Out port on the piano to the keyboard's MIDI In port. Then you select the sounds you want to use on each instrument, you play the piano, and you will hear the keyboard play along. That's all.

*This way, you can add the sound of the keyboard to what you play on the piano.*

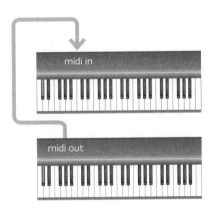

### Master

In this setup, the piano is the *master instrument*. The master instrument controls the *slave instrument*, in this case the keyboard. When you play the key C4 on the piano, MIDI tells the keyboard to do the same. It sends out a *Note On* message for the key C4. In MIDI, this key has *note number* 60.

## Velocity and Note Off

How hard you play the key is converted to a Velocity message, with a value that can vary from 1 (as softly as possible) to 127 (as loudly as possible). Thus, the keyboard will start sounding louder as you play louder, and vice versa. When you release the key, MIDI sends a Note Off message to the keyboard.

## No sound

So MIDI is about messages or *events*, not about sound. All manufacturers use the same codes for the same events. These codes and many other agreements are defined in the *MIDI protocol.*

## Control changes

The modulation wheel, for example, has been defined as *controller* #1: If you operate the modulation wheel on the master instrument, the slave instrument will respond accordingly. Likewise, you can use MIDI to send *control changes* to alter volume (controller #7), panorama or panning (#10), damper pedal (#64), effects, and so on. A *program change* is a command that instructs the slave instrument to use another sound.

## Your computer

With MIDI, you can hook up your instrument to your computer too. For that purpose, your computer needs a sound card with a MIDI interface (featuring two or more round, five-pin MIDI ports), or your instrument needs to have a USB type MIDI port (see page 134). Provided that you have the right software, you can now use your computer as a powerful sequencer, a recording studio, an interactive teacher, and much more, as you can read on pages 137–138.

## Warning

MIDI, again, is not sound. Never connect MIDI ports to an amplifier.

Front module
of a MIDI-
equipped
sound card:
MIDI in, MIDI
out, and other
connections

Front module of a MIDI-equipped sound card: MIDI in, MIDI out, and other connections

# MULTIPLE INSTRUMENTS

With MIDI, you can connect multiple instruments simultaneously. Suppose you use your piano as the master instrument, and
you want to hook up a keyboard for its beautiful strings, and a
digital organ for its great virtual tone wheel sound. To make sure
that every instrument receives the right messages, MIDI uses 16
different channels. In this specific situation, you would probably
use channel 1 to send messages to the keyboard, and channel 2 to
address the organ. If you want to use a number of different voices
on one multitimbral keyboard, you have to assign each voice to a
different channel.

### One cable
All channels travel trough the same cable, just as all your TV
channels use a single cable. You set the channel on each slave
instrument, or for each voice, just like you select a channel on your
television: Setting a channel makes it respond to the information
from that channel only.

### Thru

In addition to MIDI in and out ports, many instruments have *MIDI thru*. You use this port if you want to connect multiple instruments. MIDI Thru transmits an exact copy of the information that was received at the MIDI in port.

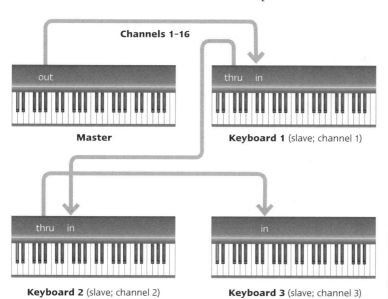

**Channels 1–16**

out | thru in
**Master** | **Keyboard 1** (slave; channel 1)

thru in | in
**Keyboard 2** (slave; channel 2) | **Keyboard 3** (slave; channel 3)

### Daisy chaining

Connecting multiple instruments by using thru ports is known as *daisy-chaining*. If you daisy-chain more than four instruments or devices, the last device may not respond properly anymore: The chain has become too long.

### MIDI thru box

This can be solved with a *MIDI splitter* or *thru box* that has a single MIDI in and multiple MIDI out ports.

### Dual ports

To prevent you from running short of channels, MIDI equipment sometimes comes with an extra set of MIDI ports. Dual ports provide you with double the number of MIDI channels (32 instead of 16).

**133**

*The computer transmits all channels to the thru box, which has an individual MIDI out for each device.*

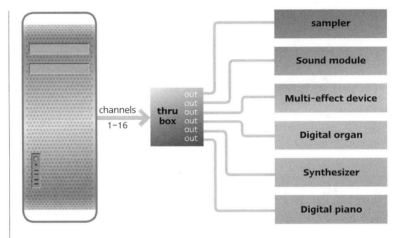

### Studio

MIDI's multiple channels are often used in studios, where a single computer can be used to control numerous different instruments, sound modules, effects, or other devices. In live situations, MIDI can also be used to synchronize lighting cues with the music.

### USB ports

A growing number of instruments uses USB type ports for MIDI, in addition to and sometimes instead of the traditional five-pin MIDI ports. This has several advantages: The computer doesn't need to have a MIDI interface, you don't need special MIDI cables, and USB ports allow for faster data transmission. The traditional MIDI ports, shown on page 130, are still used for instrument to instrument connections.

**TIP**

## MIDI to USB

*If your keyboard has five-pin MIDI connectors only, there are very affordable MIDI to USB adapters that allow you to plug it into a USB port on your computer!*

# MIDI DEVICES

There are many different devices that use MIDI, from instruments to lighting equipment, effect devices, and so on. Here are some examples.

### Sound modules

A sound module is basically an instrument without keys. You need MIDI to trigger its sound and effects. There are piano modules, organ modules, bass modules, synth modules, and so on. A sound module is a lot cheaper than the equivalent instrument with keys, of course.

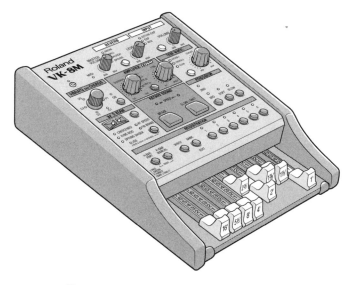

Organ module with various organ sounds, effects, drawbars, and related features. The same 'instrument' is available with a keyboard as well.

### MIDI controllers

A *MIDI controller, master keyboard,* or *controller keyboard* is the reverse of a sound module, so to speak. These 'instruments' have no sounds or effects, but they output MIDI data to trigger sounds from other MIDI devices, such as sound modules or keyboard instruments. Apart from a keyboard, they feature pitch bend and modulation wheels, and often a series of other real-time controllers, e.g., a number of assignable rotary controls that can be used to set filters, effects, volume, and so on. Small (two- or

**135**

three-octave) master keyboards have very friendly prices. When it comes to larger keyboards, an instrument with built-in sounds is often preferred.

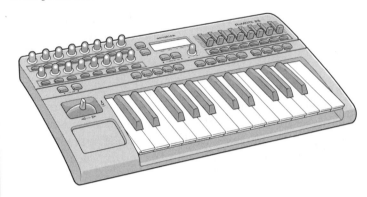

*Affordable master keyboard with a two-octave keyboard, modulation, pitch bend, and a series of assignable rotary controllers (Novation).*

### Multizone keyboards

Larger keyboard controllers often have various independent MIDI zones, which allows you to control as many MIDI devices with just one keyboard: Each zone can be assigned to a separate device.

*These MIDI wind controllers were designed for saxophonists.*

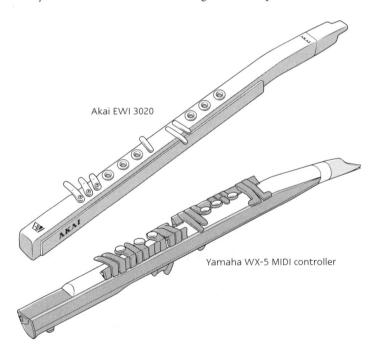

Akai EWI 3020

Yamaha WX-5 MIDI controller

### Other controllers

You don't need to be a keyboard player to use MIDI, as MIDI controllers come in other formats too, such as drum pads, MIDI guitars, or wind controllers.

### Hardware sequencers and samplers

MIDI can also be used in combination with dedicated devices such as hardware sequencers, samplers, or drum computers: big boxes that do just what their names suggest. Their popularity is decreasing as software-based versions increasingly take over their functions.

# YOUR COMPUTER

Software can turn your computer into a sequencer, an interactive teacher, a sampler, and much more. You will need dedicated software for most applications. 'Light' editions of this type of software are often included with your sound card or your instrument. Professional level software needs to be bought separately.

### Sequencers

The most popular musical application for computers is to use them as a sequencer. You can record your performance in as many steps as you have tracks available, and then edit the music, adding effects, correcting mistakes, changing the tempo, assigning other voices, and so on. With the computer's MIDI out connected to your keyboard's MIDI in, you can play back what you have created. (Most consumer oriented sound cards can play back the file too, but their built-in sound engines usually don't sound as good as your instrument.)

### Audio too

Most sequencer software doubles as a multitrack audio recorder, which turns your computer into a real digital recording studio. You can also add audio recordings (vocals, guitars, and so on) to your MIDI recordings and mix everything down to a final product that you can burn onto an audio CD-R.

*A software sequence (Cubase).*

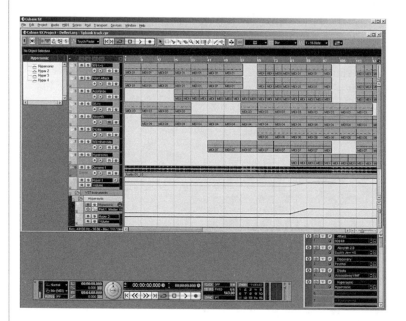

### Sampling
Computers can also be used as samplers: You can record the sound on your hard disk and play it back with your keyboard, or you can buy sample CDs or download samples from the Internet.

### Transcriptions
Computers can be used to make real-time transcriptions of your performances. You can edit the transcription and have your computer play it back. The same software can usually be used to write music too: You put the notes on the staff with your (computer) keyboard or your mouse, and you can hear what your composition sounds like right away.

### Interactive teacher
You can use your computer as an interactive teacher. There's educational software for almost any subject, from ear training to keyboard dexterity and advanced subjects such as counterpoint.

### Virtual pianos and keyboards

Similar to software sequencers and samplers, there are software pianos, organs, and synthesizers too. You play these virtual instruments with a keyboard that's connected to your computer. They're a lot cheaper than the real thing, as production costs are basically limited to copying CDs and printing the packaging.

# GENERAL MIDI

Most keyboard instruments bear a logo with the words *General MIDI*. This is a subset of agreements. One of the General MIDI or *GM* agreements is that certain voices can always be found on specified locations in the instrument's memory. If you record a song on a GM instrument, this means that this MIDI file will trigger the exact same voices if you play it back on another GM instrument: It won't sound a saxophone when it should have been a trumpet.

### Agreements

Instruments with the General MIDI logo have at least 128 different voices in specified locations; they are at least 16-part multitimbral and they have at least 24-note polyphony. Another agreement is that MIDI channel 10 is always used for drum parts.

*These logos show that the instrument is GM or GM2 compatible.*

### Level 2

GM dates back to 1991, eight years after MIDI was launched. A lot has happened since. The required number of 128 sounds, for instance, is now considered pretty low. It wasn't until 1999 that a new standard was set. This new standard, *General MIDI level 2* or *GM2*, extended the number of sounds to 256. It requires 32-note polyphony, and a lot of expressive musical parameters have

**139**

been added. Some of these *continuous controllers* are reverb time, chorus rate, chorus depth, and fine tuning. GM2 devices are fully backward compatible with older standard MIDI files.

### Proprietary formats

Quite a few manufacturers have introduced their own GM extensions, such as Roland GS, Yamaha XG and XF, and GEM GMX. These formats usually have a lot more to offer than GM or GM2, but they're not mutually compatible. However, instruments with GS or other proprietary formats can commonly play back GM files. If you play back a file that was saved as one of these extended formats on a GM instrument, you will miss some of the extra features, which range from sounds to effects and variations.

# 10

# Maintenance

*Electronic instruments require barely any maintenance,*
*but treating them well may buy you enhanced reliability*
*and a longer life expectancy.*

Electronic instruments usually have the words 'Caution, risk of electric shock' written on their housing, as well as 'Do not open — no user serviceable parts inside.' Please take these and similar messages seriously. Apart from running the risk of personal injury, tampering with an instrument will almost certainly void the guarantee.

### User's manual

Every user's manual includes a long list of things you should or shouldn't do. Please follow these guidelines carefully. And remember that this chapter doesn't replace or supersede your manual's safety instructions.

### Stands

A special keyboard stand is a worthwhile investment for portable instruments. If you plan to take your instrument on the road, find one of the many designs that collapse into a flat pack for transport.

*An easily adjustable, collapsible single-braced X-stand.*

### X-style

A very common and easily adjustable design is the X-style stand, available in single-braced and heavier double-braced models. There are other models and designs too, of course. Some offer finer height adjustment; others fold up more easily or weigh less, for example. If you want to alternate between standing up and sitting down as you play, the stand should accommodate both positions. Prices vary from less than fifty to more than two hundred dollars. Some portable keyboard instruments have a matching stand as an option (see page 51).

### Expandable stand

If you plan to use more than one instrument simultaneously, now or later, get an expandable stand that can hold two or even three instruments. Check how easily it folds up with the expansion arms attached. Tip: Some keyboard stands double as a trolley.

### Shelf-mounted

If you play at home only, you can use a wall-mounted shelf, for example. As a guide to height, the white keys of an acoustic piano are some 26" to 28" (66-72 cm) from the floor.

### Moisture

Never put drinks, vases, or any other type of liquid containers on your keyboard or piano.

### Temperature changes

Musical instruments and electronics never appreciate rapid temperature changes or extreme heat, cold, and humidity conditions. Keep your instrument away from direct sunlight, air conditioners, heating vents, fireplaces, and the like. Also be aware of the instrument's own cooling requirements, if it has any.

### Display

If it does get very warm or cold, the display may become hard to read. It should return to normal when the temperature gets less extreme.

### Static charge

Static charges can make your hair stand on end, or make sparks fly between yourself and a door handle. They can also damage electronic instruments. Apart from switching equipment on and off spontaneously, they may destroy delicate electronic components. Dry room conditions due to central heating or air conditioning often aggravate the build-up of static charges. Using a humidifier may help, and you may even try wearing shoes with leather soles.

### Radio and TV

If you use the instrument too close to a TV or a radio, it may cause interference. If so, simply move one away from the other.

### Cables

Always route cables so that they cannot be walked on or tripped over, and prevent them from being pinched by other instruments or objects. When gigging use duct tape (a.k.a. stage tape or gaffer tape) to fix cables to the floor, if possible.

### Mains and adapters

Disconnect the instrument from the mains if you're not going to be using it for a while, and disconnect the external adapter as well: It uses energy as long as it's plugged in, even when you're not playing and the instrument is turned off.

### Correct power supply

Be sure to use the correct power supply for your instrument. A 12-volt adapter may seem to work on a 9-volt instrument, but the excessive voltage may shorten its working life.

### Dust

Traditionally styled digital pianos often have a conventional keyboard cover (the fallboard or *fall*) or a sliding key cover that protects the instrument from dust, airborne pollution, and so on. Instruments that don't can always be fitted with a removable protective cover, usually available for less around twenty to forty dollars. Some covers have an adjustable cord for a snug fit.

**144**

### Key cleaning

Keys can be carefully cleaned with the a brush attachment on your vacuum cleaner. You can also use a clean, lint-free cloth. Always move from the back to the front of the keys rather than sideways. If you use a cloth, you may moisten it with a mild soap solution or some glass cleaner. Never spray any type of cleaner onto the keys. The instrument's housing can be cleaned the same way, as long as you prevent anything beneath the keys and controls from getting wet. Also check the instrument's manual for specific information. Real wood requires special care, as you can read in *Tipbook Piano* (see page 222).

### Nooks and crannies

You can use a fresh paintbrush to flick the dust from nooks and crannies. Avoid compressed-air spray cans; they just blow dust further into the instrument.

# ON THE ROAD

When on the road, a *gig bag* helps to protect your instrument from minor knocks and scratches, and it makes it a lot easier to carry.

### Things to look at

The bag should be water resistant and have solid grip handles. A shoulder strap can be very helpful. The zip should be smooth and strong. Gig bags often have one or more external zipper compartments for cables, pedals, switches, sheet music, and other accessories. Velcro fasteners inside prevent the instrument from falling out once you open the zipper. Damage of the outer skin is reduced if the bag has small rubber or metal feet, as well as corner and edge protectors. If you have a heavy instrument, consider getting a bag with wheels.

### More

Gig bag prices start around forty dollars. More money usually buys you better quality materials, heavier padding, and better zippers, among other things. Professional quality bags may cost up to two hundred.

### Flight cases

Hard-shell cases generally offer more protection than gig-bags, but they're not as easy to carry around. Size is a critical issue: The fit for keyboard instruments into hard cases should be perfect. Some models feature adjustable sizing blocks. For serious gigging and touring you'll need a genuine *flight case*, which can be custom made. Flight cases are heavy and expensive, with prices going up to four hundred dollars and more. Again, wheels may be an option.

*A gig bag with external compartments, corner protectors, Velcro fasteners inside, and a shoulder strap.*

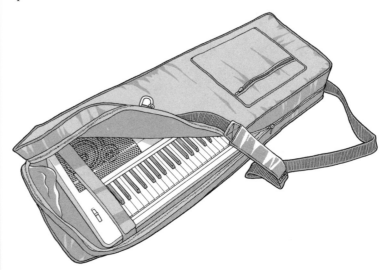

### Cables, backups, and insurance

- Always bring **spare cables** on the road — at least one of every type you use.

- Bring **backups** of USB sticks, memory cards, and other media. Also keep backups at home: Should you lose all your gear, you won't have lost all your music.

- Consider **insuring your instrument**, especially if you're taking it on the road, which includes visiting your teacher. Musical instruments fall under the 'valuables' insurance category. A

**146**

regular homeowner insurance policy will not cover all possible damage, whether it occurs at home, on the road, in the studio, or onstage.

# 11

# *History*

*This chapter briefly traces the digital piano back to its acoustic ancestor, and the home keyboard back to the organ.*

One of the earliest keyboard instruments is the *clavichord*, which was designed in the fourteenth century. *Clavis* means key; the *chords* were the instrument's strings. The working principles of the clavichord were later applied to the spinet and harpsichord: When a key is pressed, a small pick (a raven quill, actually) plucks the appropriate string.

### Pianofortes

The main drawback of these early instruments was their lack of touch sensitivity. Every note sounded equally loud. Around 1700, the Italian harpsichord maker Bartolomeo Cristofori began building an instrument that would bypass that limitation. He replaced the picks with hammers that allowed the player to play softly (*piano*, in Italian) as well as loudly (*forte*). The obvious name for this new instrument, *pianoforte*, was later shortened to piano.

*An early piano (1720) by Cristofori: four-and-a-half octaves, no pedals, and two identically tuned strings per key.*

### Today's pianos

Some twenty-five years after this introduction, Cristofori designed a new action, which already closely resembled the mechanism that is used in today's acoustic pianos.

### Electric pianos

In the late 1940s the first *electric pianos* appeared, employing short strings, metal reeds, tines, or tone bars instead of full-length strings. The vibrations were converted to electrical signals by one or more pickups, similar to the ones found on electric guitars, and then sent to an amplifier.

*Fender Rhodes Stage Piano.*

### Today

The production of electric pianos ceased in the late 1970s and early 1980s. They can still be heard today, however: either the original instruments themselves, still favored by many musicians, or sampled versions that can be found in most keyboards and digital pianos.

### Rhodes

The Fender Rhodes is probably the most popular electric piano ever. To avoid copyright problems, Rhodes-samples are often dubbed Rhodex or simply EP (electric piano), for example. The sampled sounds of the instrument vary a great deal, as the original Rhodes can be adjusted to produce a wide range of related, yet distinctly different timbres.

### Wurlitzer and Clavinet

Another popular sound is that of the Wurlitzer electric piano, used in hit albums such as Supertramp's *Crime of the Century* (1974). Hohner's Clavinet used short strings and guitar pickups. Designed as an electric alternative to the harpsichord, it became extremely popular in funk and rock bands. A famous song with a prominent role for the Clavinet is Stevie Wonder's *Superstition* (1973).

**Tipcode KEYS-018**
*Many digital pianos feature a variety of electric piano and organ sounds.*

### Electric grand

Another classic sound, Yamaha's electric grand piano (CP70, CP80), was introduced in the late 1970s, and it can still be found in the sound libraries of many keyboards and digital pianos. The electric grand had short piano strings.

### Digital pianos

In 1983, Yamaha introduced the first digital piano, and Kurzweil presented the first digital sampling keyboard.

152

# KEYBOARDS

The keyboard evolved from the organ, and the organ itself is a distant descendant of the panpipes: a row of tubes of different lengths and (thus) pitches, played the same way as you would 'play' a bottle by blowing over it. A traditional organ is basically a mechanical set of panpipes. The air stream is produced by a bellows and controlled from the keyboard. The effect of using pipes or *flutes* of different lengths to produce various timbres was later emulated by the Hammond organ's drawbars (see page 46).

### Upper and lower
Organs often have two keyboards or *manuals*, as shown in the illustration on page 155. The terms *lower manual* and *upper manual* for the left- and right-hand section of a modern keyboard stem from these dual-manual instruments.

### Electronic organ
The first electronic organs date from the 1940s. Most of them used vacuum tubes like those found in tube amplifiers and old-fashioned radios. Just like tube radios, the original tube organs were eventually replaced by transistorized *solid state* models. During the 1960s and 1970s, the electronic organ played a leading role on the keyboard market.

### One finger
The 1970s saw the arrival of the first electronic organs with primitive drum machines built in. Full accompaniment sections soon followed. A Dutch company named Riha pioneered a system that allowed entire orchestrations to be triggered with just one finger.

### Analog to digital
The first electronic organs used analog technology. Filters were applied to shape the vibrations into a wide variety of sounds, including simulations of certain instruments. Then, just as pianos went digital, so did organs. At that point, electronic organs could sound like any instrument by using samples: The (home or portable) keyboard was born.

153

### Synthesizers

The first really useful synthesizers were made in the 1960s. The most famous vintage synth is the Minimoog (1972-1980), a monophonic analog instrument that is still very popular. So popular, in fact, that an analog replica was introduced in 2002. Other companies make digital synths that emulate the 'fat' sounds of their analog predecessors of the 1970s.

*A digital simulation of an analogue synthesizer (Clavia)*

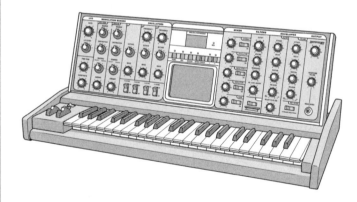

*The 2002 Minimoog Voyager.*

# TONE WHEEL ORGANS

Patented by Hammond in 1934, the Hammond tone wheel organ has a notched, rotating 2" disc for each note and a magnetic pickup for each disc. The notches produce changes in the magnetic field of the pickups, similar to what the vibrating strings of an electric guitar do. The number of notches (two for the lowest note, 256 for the highest note) determines the pitch.

154

## B-3

The B-3, Hammond's best-known model, was made from 1954 to 1974. Even though it has been digitally emulated, with designs that duplicate the original instrument at a fraction of its 400-pound weight, the vintage B-3 is still preferred over these newer models by many rock and jazz musicians.

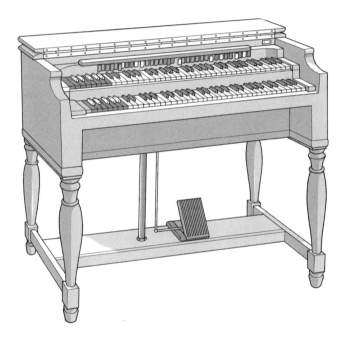

*Hammond B-3 tone wheel organ.*

## Leslie

The Hammond B-3 is hardly complete without a Leslie speaker cabinet, which has a rotating horn for the treble range and a rotating drum that swirls and projects the frequencies produced by the woofer. Since Leslie is a registered trademark, digital simulations of this effect are given alternative names such as *rotor, rotary* or *spatial sound.*

# 12

# The Family

Some of the instruments from the previous chapter are longtime members of the keyboard family. This chapter introduces some of their younger relatives.

Digital keyboard instruments can be hard to categorize. That goes for keyboards and digital pianos (and the combination of the two, the ensemble piano) as well as for synthesizers, workstations, and samplers, as you will see below.

### Synthesizers

Rather than just offer a number of preset voices, a typical synthesizer allows you to create completely original sounds. Providing you with raw samples or electronically generated tones and a wide range of filters (see page 85), a synth has all the tools you need to mold sounds into almost any shape you like.

A synthesizer
(Novation).

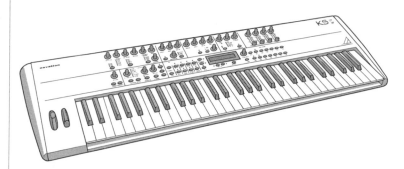

### Sample players

Other synthesizers are mainly designed to emulate the sounds of acoustic instruments. The main differences between these instruments (sometimes labeled *sample players*) and keyboards are that these synths have more sound editing capabilities.

### Workstations

A *workstation* is a self-contained compositional tool that commonly houses a large number of voices, a powerful multitrack sequencer, a large effects section, a hard disk, one or more arpeggiators, and much more. Some workstations are based on a synthesizer platform; others are closer to a home keyboard, providing you with fully editable orchestras. Workstations were originally designed to create music from scratch, but instruments that are meant for stage use are sometimes referred to as (arranger) workstations too.

**158**

### Samplers

Synths and workstations can have a built-in sampler, but there are dedicated hardware samplers too, either with or without a keyboard. Samplers usually have sound editing facilities similar to those on synths.

### All in one

A growing number of instruments combines various features in one machine, resulting in *music production synthesizers, sampling workstations, synthesizer workstations, workstation keyboards,* and so on. As said before, there are no set definitions for these terms.

### Groove machine

Another type of keyboard instrument is commonly known as *groove machine.* You can play it like a regular keyboard, but you can also use the keys as buttons that trigger preset or programmable DJ-oriented phrases, patterns, sounds, and effects, or to vary the voices that sound in a pattern so you can build it up instrument by instrument, for example. Special controllers allow you to emulate scratches or to change the pitch of a pattern without affecting the tempo, and more.

### Remote keyboards

A *remote keyboard* allows you to move around like a guitarist or a bass player, with the instrument slung around your neck. The keyboard remotely controls a MIDI sound source.

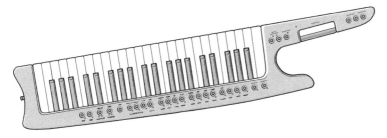

45-key remote keyboard (Roland).

### Hybrid piano

A *hybrid piano* is an acoustic piano with a (MIDI) sound module that works just like on a digital piano: The movement of the keys and pedals are registered by sensors that are connected to the

**159**

sound module. To use the digital sounds only, you lower a mute rail that stops the hammers right before they hit the strings. Beside piano samples and other voices, sound modules may also provide you with accompaniments, a CD-player or CD-burner, and a host of other features.

### Organs
Today's electronic organs and home keyboards are very similarly equipped, with a few exceptions: Organs have more organ sounds, they always come with bass pedals (see pages 50–51), and they have a volume pedal and twin keyboards — essential features for lots of organ music.

### Accordions
The *accordion* is a keyboard instrument too. The left hand usually uses small, round buttons to control a combination of bass notes and chords. The right hand, playing the melody, operates either a standard keyboard layout or a *button keyboard*, also known as *chromatic keyboards*. Accordions can be fitted with MIDI.

### Accordion keyboards
*Accordion keyboards* look like a portable keyboard instrument, but they have two separate manuals: a chromatic one for the left hand, and either a chromatic keyboard or a regular keyboard for the right hand. They're typically Italian made instruments: Italy has an impressive accordion history.

### Roll Piano
The very smallest family member is the Roll Up Piano, featuring 61 keys, 128 sounds, 100 rhythms, and MIDI. When you're done playing, you simply roll the instrument up, and off you go. The original Roll Up piano weighs about two pounds.

# 13

# Brands

*The companies in the first section of this chapter all produce a relatively wide range of keyboards and digital pianos. The companies in the second section are either smaller or have a more specialized catalog in this field.*

Please note that companies can suddenly disappear, expand, or change their production, so some of the information below may be outdated by the time you read it.

## CASIO

Since scoring a massive hit by introducing the world's first home keyboard –the VL-Tone– in 1981, Casio has focused on the lower and mid price ranges in its keyboard line. The company also makes digital pianos and a host of other electronic products, from cameras to cash registers.

*Casio VL-Tone: a miniature keyboard with ten rhythms, five sounds, and a calculator.*

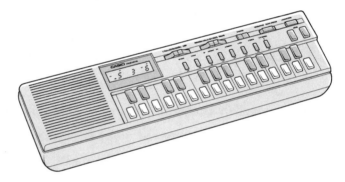

# KORG

Korg began life in the 1970s as a synthesizer manufacturer. The Japanese company makes arranger keyboards and digital pianos in the mid and high price ranges, along with workstations, synths, samplers, and related equipment.

## Roland®

Founded in Japan in 1972, Roland soon grew to be one of the world's largest manufacturers of electronic musical instruments.

162

It offers a huge choice of musical products, including all sorts of keyboard instruments, effects (under the Roland and Boss names), amplifiers, sequencers, electronic drum sets, and so on.

## YAMAHA

Yamaha started as a one-man organ factory in 1889. Besides electronic instruments and home electronics, the Japanese company produces acoustic instruments (pianos, drums, guitars, brasswinds, woodwinds, etc.) as well as sail boats, motorcycles, and much more. All products show the company's musical heritage: the logo with the three tuning forks.

## AND MORE

If you're shopping for a digital piano or a keyboard, you're bound to come across one or more instruments of the companies listed above — but they're not the only ones that make these instruments.

### Italy
Due to its accordion and organ making tradition, Italy has a relatively large number of keyboard and digital piano manu-facturers such as GEM (mentioned above), Orla, Ketron (formerly known as Solton), Viscount and Farfisa. The catalogues of Ketron and Orla include keyboards with an accordion type button keyboard. Viscount focuses on digital pianos, classic organs and sound systems. The Farfisa organs were very popular in 1960s and 1970s rock bands.

### Around the world
• In Germany, organ maker **Wersi** debuted the first keyboard with a full-blown Windows PC inside. The company also features a keyboard with real audio drum parts.

163

- **Medeli** is one of the larger Chinese companies, capable of producing some 300,000 home keyboards per year; Medeli also makes instruments for other companies listed in this chapter.

- **Kurzweil** started out as a US company producing high quality synthesizers. They also make upmarket digital pianos and grands for home and stage use, and portable keyboards.

- The **Nord** digital pianos and organs are made in Sweden.

- **M-Audio** makes a large variety of musical tools, including digital pianos and MIDI keyboards, interfaces, studio gear, and recorders.

- **Suzuki**, from Japan, produces acoustic and digital pianos, educational keyboards, and band instruments.

- **Kawai** (Japan), well known for its acoustic pianos and grands, debuted in the field of electronics in the late 1980s. The company makes digital pianos in all price ranges.

- Digital pianos are also made by companies such as **Aeolian**, **Galileo**, **Princeton**, **Samick**, **Kohler**, **Valdesta**, and **Williams**.

- **Ashton** has a modest line of Australian designed home keyboards.

# Glossary

This glossary briefly explains all the jargon touched on
so far. It also contains some terms that haven't been
mentioned yet, but which you may come across in other
books, in magazines, or on the Internet. Most terms are
explained in more detail as they are introduced in this
book. Please consult the index on pages 216–218.

Proprietary terms are not included; please refer to the
relevant manufacturer's website for information on
their meaning.

**Acc.**
See: *Auto accompaniments.*

**Acoustic piano**
Predecessor and contemporary of
the digital piano. The instrument
has a wooden housing and soundboard, 88 keys, and about 220 plain
and wound strings, which are struck
by felt-tipped wooden hammers.

**Action**
The mechanism that you operate by
depressing the keys. Very important
in how the instrument 'feels'. Digital
pianos usually have weighted or
hammered action keys, which
emulate the feel of an acoustic piano.
Most portable keyboards have non-
weighted, synth-action keys.

**ADSR**
Short for attack, decay, sustain, and
release. These four parameters make
up the *envelope* of the sound: the way
in which it builds up and tails off.
Also known as *envelope generator.*

**Aftertouch**
Allows you to manipulate the sound
by pushing the key(s) down a little
further after you've depressed them.

**Arpeggiator**
An arpeggiator generates sequences
of separate notes triggered by the
chord or the notes you play.

**Attack**
See: *ADSR.*

**Auto(matic) accompaniments**
Automatic virtual backing bands

or orchestras, usually consisting
of a rhythm section (drums, bass)
and other instruments (acc 1, acc 2,
and so on). Also labeled *accompany,
arranger, rhythm, conductor,* or *style.*

**Balance**
Control used to set the relative levels
of layered sounds, splits, the various
parts of the accompaniment, or the
left and right loudspeakers.

**Bass pedals**
Foot-operated keyboard.

**Bit depth**
Important figure in determining the
quality of samples.

**BPM**
The tempo of a piece of music is
expressed in BPM: beats per minute.

**Break**
See: *Fill.*

**CC**
Used to indicate *continuous
controller* or *control change,* both of
which refer to MIDI messages that
are used to control parameters such
as volume and effect settings.

**Channel**
MIDI uses sixteen channels. This
allows you to independently control
sixteen different instruments or
voices.

**Chord**
Three or more simultaneously
sounding notes make up a chord.
Home keyboards offer a variety of

systems that 'deduce' the right chord from your playing, using one, two, or more keys.

**Chorus**
See: *Effects*.

**Control jack**
Jack input for a controller, e.g., a volume pedal.

**Data entry wheel**
Rotary dial used to change a variety of settings. Also known as *alpha dial*, *jog wheel*, or simply *dial*.

**Delay**
See: *Effects*.

**Display**
Pianos often have small numeric displays, while those on keyboards are big enough to show the selected sounds, keys, effects, and more.

**Drawbars**
Controls that add specific overtones to the (organ) sound you play.

**DSP**
Digital Signal Processor. Generates and controls sound effects. See: *Effects*.

**Dual mode, dual voice**
See: *Layer*.

**Dynamics, dynamic range**
An instrument has good dynamics if it can play very softly, very loudly, and everywhere in between.

**Editing**
Altering sounds or MIDI files, for example.

**Effects**
Sound enhancers. Popular effects include reverb and delay (ambient effects), chorus, phasing, and flanging (modulation effects).

**Electric piano**
Predecessor of the digital piano.

**Ending**
See: *Accompaniments*.

**Ensemble piano**
Semi-generic name for digital piano with accompaniments and other features. Also known as *intelligent piano* or *rhythm piano*.

**Envelope, envelope generator**
See: *ADSR*.

**Equalizer, EQ**
Tone control, allowing you to control the timbre of the sound by boosting or cutting bass, mid, and treble, or even more specific frequency ranges.

**Event**
A (MIDI) sequencer records events, not sounds. A key going down is one event, the velocity of the key is another, and so is the release of the key, and so on.

**Expression pedal**
See: *Pedals*.

**Fader**
A sliding control, as opposed to a rotary control.

**167**

**Fill**

A short (rhythmical) variation, usually applied when going from one song section to the other. Sometimes dubbed *break*, though a break more commonly means a few counts of silence in a piece.

**Filter**

One of the main parts of a synthesizer's processing capabilities, used to shape sound. A low pass filter, for example, is used to control the amount of high frequencies in a sound by letting the low ones pass unaffected.

**General MIDI (GM)**

Addition to the original MIDI standard, containing specific assignments of sound numbers, channels, and more. See also: *MIDI*.

**GM**

See: *General MIDI.*

**Grand piano**

Acoustic piano with a horizontal (as opposed to vertical or upright) soundboard and strings.

**Hammer(ed) action**

See: *Action.*

**Hammond organ**

Electric organ with spinning tone wheels.

**Hybrid piano**

Acoustic piano with a built-in sound module.

**Jack**

Connector.

**Keyboard**

A word with many meanings. First and foremost, it is used to designate the common controller of all keyboard instruments, also known as the *manual*. Secondly, it is used to indicate the type of electronic keyboard musical instrument that has an auto accompaniment system. Thirdly, it may indicate any or all instruments that have a keyboard, from grand pianos to synthesizers.

**Keys**

Instruments can have waterfall keys, piano-style/box-type keys, or overhanging/synth-type keys.

**Layer**

The *layer* feature allows you to stack two or more sounds on top of each other. Also known as *dual mode* or *dual voice.*

**Lower, lower manual**

Indicates the left side of the keyboard; upper indicates the right side. Stems from organs that have two keyboards, an upper one a lower one. See also: *Split.*

**Manual**

1. Another word for the keyboard of an instrument.
2. Virtually indispensable handbook for most keyboard instruments.

**Master instrument**

The instrument that you use to control other instruments or devices.

**168**

**Memory**
All data (e.g., sounds, styles, the operating system) are stored in digital memory. There are two basic types of memory: ROM and RAM. Data in RAM (*Random Access Memory*) can be edited. Data in ROM (*Read Only Memory*) can't.

**Metronome**
A device that emits beeps or clicks to state the tempo. Usually built-in.

**MIDI**
Short for Musical Instrument Digital Interface. Allows digital instruments and other equipment to communicate with each other.

**MIDI file**
See: *Standard MIDI file.*

**MIDI in, MIDI out, MIDI thru**
Connections for receiving, transmitting, and retransmitting MIDI information respectively.

**Modulation**
1. A modulation wheel is a control commonly used to make the sound vibrate (a slight rapid alternation of the pitch).
2. Chorus, flanger, and phaser are commonly known as modulation effects.

**Multimedia keyboard**
Home keyboard with TV and/or monitor connections.

**Multitimbral**
A multitimbral instrument is able to produce several different sounds at the same time. Many keyboards are 16-part multitimbral.

**Multitrack**
See: *Track.*

**Note number**
For MIDI purposes, every pitch has a note number assigned to it.

**Octave**
Twelve consecutive white and black keys make up an octave. The size of a keyboard is often expressed as the number of octaves it covers.

**Pitch bend**
A feature allowing you to bend the pitch of the notes up or down, usually controlled by a wheel or a joystick.

**Polyphonic**
A 96-voice polyphonic instrument is capable of sounding 96 notes (voices) simultaneously. Early synthesizers were monophonic: They produced a single note at a time.

**Preset**
You can store sounds, styles, or other data under one or more presets. Factory presets are pre-programmed by the manufacturer of the instrument. User presets can be modified by the user.

**Quantizing**
Sequencers record events in 'steps,' distributing the notes in a timing grid. The finer this grid, the higher the quantize resolution (expressed in ppq; pulses per quarter note), and the more accurate the recording.

**169**

A low quantize resolution can be used to solve timing problems when recording. See also: *Resolution.*

**RAM**
See: *Memory.*

**Real-time controller**
Allows you to change volume, effect settings, and other elements in real time, i.e., while you're playing.

**Release velocity**
Lets you control the sound by how fast you let the keys return to their original position.

**Resolution**
The higher the resolution, the better the sequencer records your timing subtleties. Thrown in a wheelbarrow, a load of bricks will roughly take on the shape of the barrow. A load of sand will do so far more accurately. In other words, sand has a higher 'resolution' than bricks.

**Reverb**
See: *Effects.*

**Ribbon controller**
Controller operated by sliding a finger over it.

**ROM**
See: *Memory.*

**Sample**
Digitally recorded sound.

**Sampler**
A device to record, manipulate, and play back samples. See also: *Sample.*

**Sampling rate**
Important figure in determining the quality of samples.

**Sequencer**
Digital recorder of electronic musical events, as opposed to a recorder of sounds. Keyboard instruments usually have one on board.

**SMF**
See: *Standard MIDI File.*

**Soft keys**
Control buttons on the perimeter of a display, used to select items from information in the display. As the information changes, so do the functions of the buttons.

**Sound module**
You can expand your instrument with sound modules, which offer additional sounds and other features.

**Split**
Allows you to use different sounds on the left (lower) and right (upper) side of the keyboard.

**Stage piano**
Digital piano designed for onstage use. Usually lacks built-in speakers.

**Stand**
Most keyboard stands have an X-shaped design.

**Standard MIDI File (SMF)**
Most sequencers can read and save Standard MIDI files. Standard MIDI

files can have various formats, e.g., General MIDI, XS, and GX.

**Synthesizer**
Electronic musical instrument designed to create, program, manipulate, and play sounds.

**Touch sensitivity**
An instrument with a touch sensitive keyboard sounds louder the harder you strike the keys, and vice versa. Also referred to as *touch response* and *velocity sensitivity.*

**Track**
1. Each part of an accompaniment (drums, bass, violins, etc.) is assigned to a separate track.
2. Most sequencers have multiple tracks to allow several parts to be recorded independently of each other and played back simultaneously. This is known as multitracking.

**Transpose**
By transposing an instrument's pitch, you can make it sound higher or lower (in half tone steps, up to one or more octaves).

**Tuning**
Most instruments can have their overall pitch finely adjusted up or down a small amount. Some digital pianos can be tuned one key at a time, just like acoustic ones.

**Upper, upper manual**
See: *Lower, lower manual.*

**Velocity**
See: *Touch sensitive.*

**Vibrato**
See: *Modulation.*

**Waterfall keys**
See: *Keys.*

**WAV-file**
Common format to save audio files.

**Weighted keyboard**
See: *Action.*

**Workstation**
Electronic musical instrument that commonly houses samples, a sequencer, effects, a disk drive, an arpeggiator, and many other features.

# Tipcode List

The Tipcodes in this book offer easy access to short videos, sound files, and other additional information at www.tipbook.com. For your convenience, the Tipcodes in this Tipbook have been listed below.

# Want to Know More?

*Tipbooks supply you with basic information on the instrument of your choice, and everything that comes with it. Of course there's a lot more to be found on all of the subjects you came across on these pages. This section offers a selection of magazines, books, helpful websites, and more.*

## MAGAZINES

Reviews of keyboards, digital pianos, and related equipment can be found in various general music magazines. A few specialized magazines also feature articles and news on electronic instruments and related gear and subjects.

- *Keyboard*, www.keyboardmag.com

- *Electronic Musician*, www.emusician.com (personal music production)

- *Sound On Sound* (UK), www.sospubs.co.uk (electronic instruments and recording)

- *Keyboard Player Magazine* (UK), www.keyboardplayer.com

- *Computer Music* (UK), www.computermusic.co.uk (making music with computers)

- *Future Music* (UK), www.futuremusic.co.uk (hardware and software)

## BOOKS

Books dedicated to home/portable keyboards and digital pianos are very rare, but there are many titles on a wide variety of related subjects, from MIDI to sampling, synthesizers, and computer music. Following are some samples. Always check for new editions!

- *Choosing and Using Audio and Music Software: A guide to the major software applications for Mac and PC*, by Mike Collins (2004).

- *How MIDI Works*, by Peter Lawrence Alexander (2001).

- *Making Music with Your Computer*, by Brent Edstrom (2000).

- *MIDI Power!*, Second Edition: The Comprehensive Guide (Power!), by Robert Guerin (2005).

- *Music Technology Workbook: Key concepts and practical projects*, by Paul Middleton and Steven Gurevitz (2007).

- *Quick Start: MIDI*, by Reinhard Schmitz (2003).

- *Sound On Sound: Midi For Technophobe*, by Paul White (2004).

- *The Art of Digital Music: 56 Visionary Artists and Insiders Reveal Their Creative Secrets*, by David Battino and Stewart Copeland (2004).

- *The MIDI Manual, Third Edition: A Practical Guide to MIDI in the Project Studio*, by David Miles Huber (2007).

- *The S.M.A.R.T. Guide to Producing Music with Samples, Loops, and MIDI*, by Bill A. Gibson (2005).

- *What's MIDI?: Making Musical Instruments Work Together*, by Jon F. Eiche and Emile Menasche (2001).

### INTERNET

There's a vast amount of online information on digital keyboard instruments, MIDI, and related subjects. Below are some relevant websites on various subjects. Most manufacturers have an informative website too.

- Classical MIDI connection: www.classicalmidiconnection.com

- Electronic Music Foundation: www.emf.org

- Harmony Central: www.harmonycentral.com

- Loops: www.loops.net

- MIDI.com: www.midi.com

- MIDI Farm: www.midifarm.com

- Music Machines: machines.hyperreal.org

- Sample Net: www.samplenet.com

### LOOKING FOR A TEACHER?

If you want to find a teacher online, try searching for "keyboard teacher" or "piano teacher" and the name of area or city where you live, or visit one of the following special interest websites:

- PrivateLessons.com: www.privatelessons.com

- MusicStaff.com: www.musicstaff.com

- The Music Teachers List: www.teachlist.com

# Chord Charts

One of the great things about a keyboard instrument is that it allows you to play chords. On a piano, you have to play all the notes of a chord yourself. On a home keyboard there are various ways to make it easier for you to play chords, as explained on pages 115–117. In both cases it's good to know a little more about the way chords are constructed and executed on your instrument.

Songbooks and most songs that you can download from the internet come with chord symbols that tell you which chords to play. It takes time to learn how to translate some of these symbols to the actual notes that you should use. The numerous chord charts on pages 190–213 help you out. Of course, both basic and advanced chords are included.

### Chord construction

Reading chord symbols becomes a lot easier if you know how chords are constructed. This not only allows to understand which notes to play; it also gives you some insight in what chords can do and what you can do with them, such as playing inversions (see pages 188–189). For keyboard players, this knowledge allows you to play the notes of the chords yourself rather than having your instrument figuring them out for you.

### Improvisation

If you play a solo over a chord progression, the notes of the chords offer you a safe starting point for your improvisation. For an advanced level of playing, you should of course also know the scales that those chords are based on. This goes beyond the scope of this section, so scales are not included here.

### Chord charts

The chord charts in this book show chords that are made up of three, four, and five or more notes. Every root note (C, C♯, D, etc.) has a double page, starting with the most basic chords (three pitches) on the left.

### Four groups

The chord charts are presented in four main groups, from the top to the bottom of the page:

- **Major chords**: chords with a major third (3).

- **Minor chords**: chords with a minor third (♭3).

- **Dominant chords**: chords with a major third and a minor seventh (♭7)

- **Diminished chords**: chords with a minor third (♭3) and a diminished fifth (♭5).

### Variations

Each main group of chords includes a number of variations, such as major chords with lowered or raised pitches (e.g., ♭5 or ♯5).

### Chord symbols

Most chords can be indicated with various chord symbols. The chord charts list one symbol per chord. Most other chord symbols can be found in the table on pages 180–183, which also includes the construction of the various types of chords and their full names

### Steps

The table also shows the *scale degrees* or *steps* of each type of chord. For example, a major chord is made up of the degrees 1–3–5: the root note (1, also indicated as R), a major third (3) and a perfect fifth (5). These scale degrees are also used throughout the text on the following pages. In most cases, the text also includes an example of the chord in actual pitches, using C chords most of the time.

### Intervals

To take full advantage of this section of the book, you should have a fair knowledge of basic music theory, including the intervals and accidentals (sharps and flats). If you don't, please check out *Tipbook Music On Paper* (see page 222).

# CHORD CONSTRUCTION

How are chords constructed? The basic principle is quite straight-forward. Here's the C major chord.

- The root note is the first note (1) of a chord. In C major that's a C.

- The second pitch sounds a major third (3) higher. In C major that's an E.

- The third pitch sounds a perfect fifth (5) higher than the root note. In C major that's a G.

179

| Chord symbol | Alternative symbols | Pitches (C) |
|---|---|---|
| **Major** | | |
| C | – | C, E, G |
| Csus4 | – | C, F, G |
| C2 | – | C, D, E, G |
| Csus2 | – | C, D, G |
| C6 | – | C, E, G, A |
| Cmaj7 | C$\Delta$ | C, E, G, B |
| C6/9 | – | C, E, G, A, D |
| Cmaj7$^9$ | C$\Delta^9$ | C, E, G, B, D |
| C$\flat$5 | – | C, E, G$\flat$ |
| Caug | C+ | C, E, G$\sharp$ |
| C$\sharp$4 | – | C, E, F$\sharp$, G |
| Cmaj7$^{\sharp5}$ | C$\Delta^{\sharp5}$ | C, E, G$\sharp$, B |
| Cmaj7$^{\flat5}$ | C$\Delta^{\flat5}$ | C, E, G$\flat$, B |
| Cmaj7$^{\sharp11}$ | C$\Delta^{\sharp11}$ | C, E, G, B, F$\sharp$ |
| Cmaj7$^{9\,\sharp11}$ | C$\Delta^{9\,\sharp11}$ | C, E, G, B, D, F$\sharp$ |
| Cmaj7$^{\flat6}$ | C$\Delta^{\flat6}$ | C, E, G, A$\flat$, B |
| Cmaj7$^{9\,\flat6}$ | C$\Delta^{9\,\flat6}$ | C, E, G, A$\flat$, B, D |
| Cmaj7$^{9\,13}$ | C$\Delta^{9\,13}$ | C, E, G, B, D, A |
| Cmaj7$^{9\,\sharp1113}$ | C$\Delta^{9\,\sharp1113}$ | C, E, G, B, D, F$\sharp$, A |
| **Minor** | | |
| Cmin | C–, Cm | C, E$\flat$, G |
| Cmin2 | C–2, Cm2 | C, D, E$\flat$, G |
| Cmin6 | C–6, Cm6 | C, E$\flat$, G, A |
| Cmin7 | C–7, Cm7 | C, E$\flat$, G, B$\flat$ |
| Cmin$^{maj7}$ | C$^{-maj7}$, Cm$^{maj7}$, C–$\Delta$, Cm$\Delta$ | C, E$\flat$, G, B |
| Cmin7$^{\flat5}$ | C–7$^{\flat5}$, Cm7$^{\flat5}$, C$\varnothing$ | C, E$\flat$, G$\flat$, B$\flat$ |
| Cmin6/9 | C–6$^9$, Cm6$^9$ | C, E$\flat$, G, A, D |
| Cmin7$^9$ | C–7$^9$, Cm7$^9$ | C, E$\flat$, G, B$\flat$, D |
| Cmin$^{maj7\,9}$ | C$^{-maj7\,9}$, Cm$^{maj7\,9}$ | C, E$\flat$, G, B, D |
| Cmin7$^{9\,\flat5}$ | C–7$^{9\,\flat5}$, Cm7$^{9\,\flat5}$ | C, E$\flat$, G$\flat$, B$\flat$, D |
| Cmin7$^{\flat6}$ | C–7$^{\flat6}$, Cm7$^{\flat6}$ | C, E$\flat$, G, A$\flat$, B$\flat$ |
| Cmin7$^{9\,\flat6}$ | C–7$^{9\,\flat6}$, Cm7$^{9\,\flat6}$ | C, E$\flat$, G, A$\flat$, B$\flat$, D |
| Cmin7$^{\flat9\,11(omit3)}$ | C$^{-\flat9\,11(omit3)}$, Cm$^{\flat9\,11(omit3)}$ | C, G, B$\flat$, D$\flat$, F, A |
| **Diminished** | | |
| Cdim | C° | C, E$\flat$, G$\flat$, A |
| Cdim7 | C°7 | C, E$\flat$, G$\flat$, A, B |

| Steps (1 = R) | Full name |
|---|---|
| 1, 3, 5 | C major |
| 1, 4, 5 | C suspended (four) |
| 1, 2, 3, 5 | C two |
| 1, 2, 5 | C suspended (two) |
| 1, 3, 5, 6 | C six |
| 1, 3, 5, 7 | C major seven |
| 1, 3, 5, 6, 9 | C six nine |
| 1, 3, 5, 7, 9 | C major seven nine |
| 1, 3, ♭5 | C half-diminished |
| 1, 3, ♯5 | C augmented |
| 1, 3, ♯4, 5 | C sharp four |
| 1, 3, ♯5, 7 | C major seven sharp five |
| 1, 3, ♭5, 7 | C major seven flat five |
| 1, 3, 5, 7, ♯11 | C major seven sharp eleven |
| 1, 3, 5, 7, 9, ♯11 | C major seven nine sharp eleven |
| 1, 3, 5, ♭6, 7 | C major seven flat six |
| 1, 3, 5, ♭6, 7, 9 | C major seven nine flat six |
| 1, 3, 5, 7, 9, 13 | C major seven nine thirteen |
| 1, 3, 5, 7, 9, ♯11, 13 | C major seven nine sharp eleven thirteen |

| Steps (1 = R) | Full name |
|---|---|
| 1, ♭3, 5 | C minor |
| 1, 2, ♭3, 5 | C minor two |
| 1, ♭3, 5, 6 | C minor six |
| 1, ♭3, 5, ♭7 | C minor seven |
| 1, ♭3, 5, 7 | C minor/major seven |
| 1, ♭3, ♭5, ♭7 | C half-diminished |
| 1, ♭3, 5, 6, 9 | C minor six nine |
| 1, ♭3, 5, ♭7, 9 | C minor seven nine |
| 1, ♭3, 5, 7, 9 | C minor/major seven nine |
| 1, ♭3, ♭5, ♭7, 9 | C minor seven flat five |
| 1, ♭3, 5, ♭6, ♭7 | C minor seven flat six |
| 1, ♭3, 5, ♭6, ♭7, 9 | C minor seven nine flat six |
| 1, 5, ♭7, ♭9, 11 | C minor seven flat nine eleven omit three |

| Steps (1 = R) | Full name |
|---|---|
| 1, ♭3, ♭5, 6 | C diminished |
| 1, ♭3, ♭5, 6, 7 | C diminished seven |

| Chord symbol | Alternative symbols | Pitches (C) |
|---|---|---|
| **Dominant** | | |
| C7 | – | C, E, G, B♭ |
| C7sus4 | C11 | C, F, G, B♭ |
| C7♭5 | – | C, E, G♭, B♭ |
| C7♭9 | C9 | C, E, G, B♭, D |
| C7♭9 sus4 | – | C, F, G, B♭, D |
| C7♭9 ♯5 | – | C, E, G♯, B♭, D |
| C7♭9 ♭6 | – | C, E, G, A♭, B♭, D |
| C7♭9 ♯11 | – | C, E, G, B♭, D, F♯ |
| C7♭9 | – | C, E, G, B♭, D♭ |
| C7♭5 ♭9 | – | C, E, G♭, B♭, D♭ |
| C7♭9 ♯11 | – | C, E, G, B♭, D♭, F♯ |
| C7♯9 | – | C, E, G, B♭, D♯ |
| C7♯9 ♯11 | – | C, E, G, B♭, D♯, F♯ |
| C7♭5 ♯9 | C7alt | C, E, G♯, B♭, D♯ |
| C7♭5 ♯9 ♯11 | C7alt | C, E, G♯, B♭, D♯, F♯ |
| C7♭9 13 | – | C, E, G, B♭, D, A |
| C7♭9 ♯11 13 | – | C, E, G, B♭, D, F♯, A |
| C7♭9 13 | – | C, E, G, B♭, D♭, A |
| C7♭9 ♯11 13 | – | C, E, G, B♭, D♭, F♯, A |
| C7♯9 ♯11 13 | – | C, E, G, B♭, D♯, F♯, A |
| C7♯9 ♯11 ♭13 | C7alt | C, E, G, B♭, D♯, F♯, A♭ |
| C7sus4 9 13 | – | C, E, F, B♭, D, A |
| C7sus4 ♭9 13 | – | C, E, F, B♭, D♭, A |

### Major (continued from page 179)

So the C major chord consists of the pitches C–E–G. Just like any other major chord, its steps are 1–3–5 of R–3–5.

### Minor

In a minor chord, the second pitch is a minor third, so C minor has the pitches C–E♭–G. All minor chords have the following construction: R–♭3–5. The flat (♭) lowers the third a half step.

### Augmented

An augmented chord is made up of two major thirds: R–3–♯5. The sharp (♯) raises the fifth a half step. C augmented consists of the notes C–E–G♯.

| Steps (1 = R) | Full name |
|---|---|
| 1, 3, 5, ♭7 | C seven / C dominant seven |
| 1, 4, 5, ♭7 | C seven suspended four |
| 1, 3, ♭5, ♭7 | C seven flat five |
| 1, 3, 5, ♭7, 9 | C seven nine |
| 1, 4, 5, ♭7, 9 | C seven nine suspended four |
| 1, 3, ♯5, ♭7, 9 | C seven nine sharp five |
| 1, 3, 5, ♭6, ♭7, 9 | C seven nine flat six |
| 1, 3, 5, ♭7, 9, ♯11 | C seven nine sharp eleven |
| 1, 3, 5, b7, b9 | C seven flat nine |
| 1, 3, ♭5, ♭7, ♭9 | C seven flat five flat nine |
| 1, 3, 5, ♭7, ♭9, ♯11 | C seven flat nine sharp eleven |
| 1, 3, 5, ♭7, ♯9 | C seven sharp nine |
| 1, 3, 5, ♭7, ♯9, ♯11 | C seven sharp nine sharp eleven |
| 1, 3, ♯5, ♭7, ♯9 | C seven sharp five sharp nine |
| 1, 3, ♯5, ♭7, ♯9, ♯11 | C seven sharp five sharp nine sharp eleven |
| 1, 3, 5, ♭7, 9, 13 | C seven nine thirteen |
| 1, 3, 5, ♭7, 9, ♯11, 13 | C seven nine sharp eleven thirteen |
| 1, 3, 5, ♭7, ♭9, 13 | C seven flat nine thirteen |
| 1, 3, 5, ♭7, ♭9, ♯11, 13 | C seven flat nine sharp eleven thirteen |
| 1, 3, 5, ♭7, ♯9, ♯11, 13 | C seven sharp nine sharp eleven thirteen |
| 1, 3, 5, ♭7, ♯9, ♯11, ♭13 | C seven sharp nine sharp eleven flat thirteen |
| 1, 3, 4, ♭7, 9, 13 | C seven suspended four nine thirteen |
| 1, 3, 4, ♭7, ♭9, 13 | C seven suspended four flat nine thirteen |

## Stacked thirds

_TIP_

*Chords basically consist of stacked thirds. (They're known as tertial chords.) A major chord consists of a major third (1–3) and a minor third (3–5). In a minor chord, the order of these thirds is inverted: 1–♭3 is a minor third, and ♭3–5 is a major third. A diminished chord has two minor thirds — and so on.*

### Four

All chords mentioned so far consist of three pitches. There are also chords with four or more pitches. Those extra notes, known as

**183**

*extensions*, are typically indicated by adding numbers (steps) to the chord symbol.

- An added 7 indicates that a minor seven should be added: The chord C7 (a **dominant** or dominant 7 chord) consists of the notes C–E–G–B♭ (R–3–5–♭7). Together, the 3 and the ♭7 make this chord sound a bit bluesy.

- If maj7 is added to the root note (e.g., Cmaj7), the fourth pitch is a major seven. **C major 7** consists of the pitches C–E–G–B (R–3–5–7).

- The 6 in a **major 6** chord adds a major six to the chord. For example, C6 is C–E–G–A (R–3–5–6).

- A **9** in a C chord adds a high D to the chord

- A ♭**9** adds a lowered nine (D♭); a ♯**9** adds a raised nine (D♯).

- You can also add an **11** or a **13**, for example.

### The same pitch

In other countries, ♯9 is sometimes indicated as ♭10. These notes sound exactly the same pitch (in C, they're D♯ and E♭). In a chord, these notes have the same function, as they sound the same pitch, just like a raised four sounds the same pitch (F♯, in the key of C) as a lowered five (G♭).

---

**Double sharp, double flat**

In some chords, raised or lowered notes need to be raised or lowered once more. For example, turning F♯ major (F♯–A♯–C♯) into an F♯ augmented chord raises the C♯ once more. Officially, this turns it into a C double-sharp. In daily use — and in this book — however, this tone is indicated by the name of the pitch that it sounds, the D. Likewise, a raised B is called a C, rather than a B sharp (B) .

---

### No 13 and ♭13

The chord diagrams in this sections show the main chords with extensions up to and including ♯11; 13 and ♭13 are not included.

**184**

*Tip:* In chord symbols, ♭13 is sometimes written as ♯5. If so, you're looking at an *altered* chord: a chord in which all pitches except 1 and 3 have been altered. Below are some examples of chords with an added 13. The knowledge on the previous pages allows you to construct these chords for other root notes too. Some 13 and ♭13 chords are also included in the table on pages 180–183.

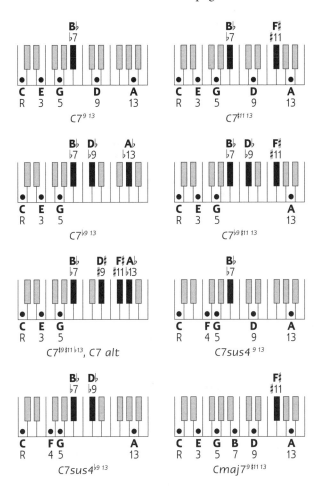

## Not required

Extensions add color and character to a chord — but you're not required to play all of them at all times. If you're accompanying a soloist, for example, it's typically sufficient to play the R, 3, 5, and

7 of a given chord. So if the chord symbol reads C7$^{\flat9\sharp11}$, for example, you can simply play C7.

### Leave out other pitches

You can also choose to leave out other pitches, as long as you realize that the character or timbre of a chord is mainly determined by its 3 and 7. If you play in a band, you can usually leave out the root note; the bass player will play this note. The 5 can often be omitted too. In the chord charts on pages 190–213, the pitches that can be left out are marked grey (for chords made up of five or more pitches only).

*You can leave out the grey keys.*

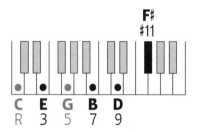

### Add pitches

You may also want to add pitches to a chord. For example, a 9 can be great addition to a maj7 chord (R–3–5–7–9).

### Two hands

Chords that are made up of four or more pitches are easier to play if you use both hands — and you can do so to for chords with three pitches, of course. Using both hands allows you to spread the notes over the keyboard (*open voicings*) rather than playing them close together (*closed voicings*). More tips:

• If you use both hands, it may be tempting to double play certain notes— but you shouldn't, except maybe for the 7. **Doubling the 7** helps to enhance the chord.

• Experiment with **closed and open voicings**. For example, play the 1 (C) of Cmaj7 with your left hand, and play 3, 5 and 7 to the right.

• Is there a **bass player onstage**? Leave the root note of that chord out, play the 3 with your left hand, and use your right hand for the 5 and the 7. You may consider adding a 9 to the chord, as suggested earlier; play it between the 3 and the 5, in this particular case.

### Omit

Sometimes, the composer or arranger tells you which pitches to leave out, adding the word 'omit' to the chord symbol. The illustration at the bottom of this page shows you an example. The opposite also happens, using the word 'add' to indicate an extra extension. For example, you normally would not play the 3 in a C7sus4 chord, but it can sound really nice. If the composer wants you to add that 3, the chord symbol will read C7sus4(add3). Actually, this 3 is a bit misleading as you're supposed to play it as an additional higher note, the 10: both the 3 and the 10 are an E, in this chord. Played with two hands, this chord looks like this:

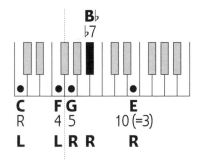

*C7sus4*(add3)
*played with two
hands*

### Extensions and alternatives

You can opt for a closed voicing by replacing chord extensions. For example, you may play a ♯4 rather than a ♯11 (in a C chord, both are F♯s), or replace a ♭9 by a ♭2. As you may have noted, it's simply a

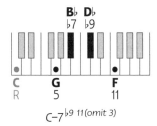

C–7♭9 11(omit 3)

Played as the chord symbol
suggests.

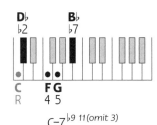

C–7♭9 11(omit 3)

Replacing ♭9 (D♭) by a ♭2 and
the 11 (F) by a 4 (right).

**187**

matter of subtracting 7 (11=4, 9=2, etc.). Still, you're usually supposed to play the extensions at their original pitches, i.e., higher than the other notes of the chord — but some chords tend to sound better if you don't. An example of such a chord, $7^{9\ 11(\text{omit3})}$, is shown on the previous page.

# INVERSIONS

You can play the pitches of a chord in any order you like. If the root note is the lowest pitch of the chord, you're playing the chord in its *root position* (R–3–5).

*C major: root position and first and second inversions.*

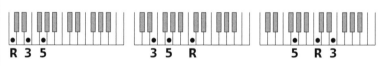

R 3 5          3 5 R          5 R 3

Root position       first inversion       second inversion

- If you make the 3 the lowest pitch, you're playing the first inversion: 3–5–R.

- The second inversion starts with the 5 as the lowest pitch: 5–R–3.

### Easier

Inversions can make it a lot easier to go from one chord to the other. For example, you need to really 'jump' when you go from C major to G major in their root positions. Now play C major in its second inversion (G–C–E), and go to G major (G–B–D): all you have to do is move two fingers. Apart from being easier, this sounds better too. As a general rule: If the next chord has one or two notes in common with the previous chord, play them on the same keys. The less you move, the easier it will be and the better you will sound.

### More pitches

Additional pitches allow for additional inversions, of course. In a

**188**

major7 chord, for example, the root position would be R–3–5–7, followed by the first inversion (3–5–7–R), the second (5–7–R–3), and the third inversion (7–R–3–5).

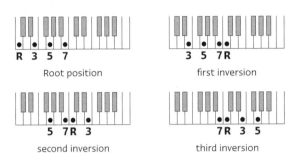

R 3 5 7
Root position

3 5 7R
first inversion

5 7R 3
second inversion

7R 3 5
third inversion

*Cmaj7: root position and first, second, and third inversions.*

### Example

Here's another example of how inverting chords can help you sound better and play easier. If you look at the two chords below, you will see that they have the notes G and B in common, so you should invert the chords in a way that allows you to keep your fingers on those two keys.

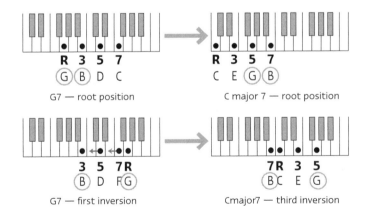

R 3 5 7
G B D C
G7 — root position

R 3 5 7
C E G B
C major 7 — root position

3 5 7R
B D F♯ G
G7 — first inversion

7R 3 5
B C E G
Cmajor7 — third inversion

*Two ways to go from G7 to C major 7. Inverting both chords makes things a lot easier.*

### Online

Final tip: Check the internet for additional piano chord charts. The Big Bands Database Plus (http://nfo.net/mfile) and Hot Bands (www.hotbands.com/pianochart.php) are two great starting points.

**189**

# C

## Inversions

### Three-note chords

Root position

R 3 5

First inversion

3 5 R

Second inversion

5 R 3

### Four-note chords

Root position

R 3 5 7

First inversion

3 5 7R

Second inversion

5 7R 3

Third inversion

7R 3 5

---

### Three-note chords

#### Major

C E G
R 3 5

C

#### Major with ♭5 / ♯5

G♭
♭5
C E
R 3

C♭5

G♯
♯5
C E
R 3

Caug

#### Minor

E♭
♭3
C G
R 5

Cmin

#### Diminished

E♭ G♭
♭3 ♭5
C
R

Cdim

---

### Four-note chords

#### Major

C D E G
R 2 3 5

Csus2, C2

C E G A
R 3 5 6

C6

C E G B
R 3 5 7

Cmaj7

#### Major chords with accidentals

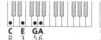

F♯
♯4
C F G
R 4 5

Csus4

G♯
♯5
C E G
R 3 5

C♯4

G♭
♭5
C E B
R 3 7

Cmaj7♯5

G♭
♭5
C E B
R 3 7

Cmaj7♭5

#### Minor

E♭
♭3
C D G
R 2 5

Cmin2

E♭
♭3
C G A
R 5 6

Cmin6

E♭ B♭
♭3 ♭7
C G
R 5

Cmin7

#### Minor chords with accidentals

E♭
♭3
C G B
R 5 7

Cmin^maj7

E♭ G♭ B♭
♭3 ♭5 ♭7
C
R

Cmin7♭5

#### Dominant

B♭
♭7
C E G
R 3 5

C7

B♭
♭7
C F G
R 4 5

C7sus4

#### Dominant chords with accidentals

G♭ B♭
♭5 ♭7
C E
R 3

C7♭5

#### Diminished

E♭ G♭
♭3 ♭5
C A
R 6

Cdim

# C

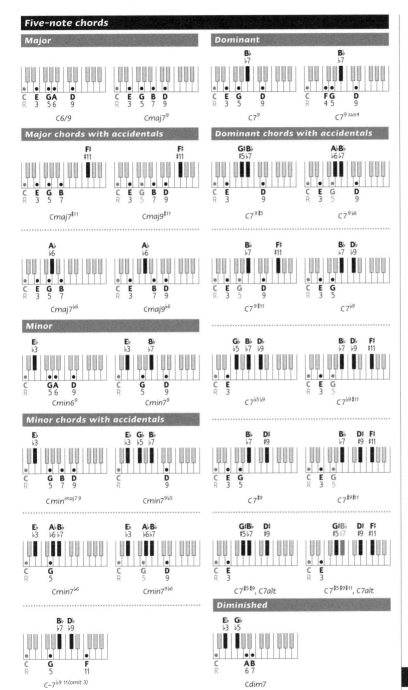

## Five-note chords

### Major

C6/9

Cmaj7⁹

### Major chords with accidentals

Cmaj7♯11

Cmaj9♯11

Cmaj7♭6

Cmaj9♭6

### Minor

Cmin6⁹

Cmin7⁹

### Minor chords with accidentals

Cmin^maj7 9

Cmin7⁹♭5

Cmin7♭6

Cmin7⁹♭6

C−7♭9 11(omit 3)

### Dominant

C7⁹

C7⁹ sus4

### Dominant chords with accidentals

C7⁹♯5

C7⁹♭6

C7⁹♯11

C7♭9

C7♭5♭9

C7♭9♯11

C7♯9

C7♯9♯11

C7♯5♯9, C7alt

C7♯5♯9♯11, C7alt

### Diminished

Cdim7

● Play these keys.

◐ Can be left out.

| | |
|---|---|
| ♭9 | = ♭2 |
| 9 | = 2 |
| ♯9 | = ♭10 |
| 11 | = 4 |
| ♯11 | = ♯4 |
| ♯11 | = ♭5 |
| ♭13 | = ♯5 |
| 13 | = 6 |
| ♭13 | = ♭6 |

# D♭

*Enharmonic: C♯*

## Inversions

### Three-note chords

Root position:
R-3-5

First inversion:
3-5-R

Second inversion:
5-R-3

### Four-note chords

Root position:
R-3-5-7

First inversion:
3-5-7-R

Second inversion:
5-7-R-3

Third inversion:
7-R-3-5

## Three-note chords

### Major

D♭

D♭sus4

### Major with ♯ or ♭

D♭♭5

### Minor

D♭min

### Diminished

D♭dim

## Four-note chords

### Major

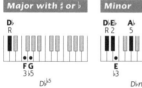

D♭sus2, D♭2        D♭6        D♭maj7

### Major chords with accidentals

D♭♯4        D♭maj7♯5        D♭maj7♭5

### Minor

D♭min2        D♭min6        D♭min7

### Minor chords with accidentals

D♭aug        D♭min^maj7        D♭min7♭5

### Dominant

D♭7        D♭7sus4

### Dominant chords with accidentals

D♭7♭5

### Diminished

D♭dim

# D♭

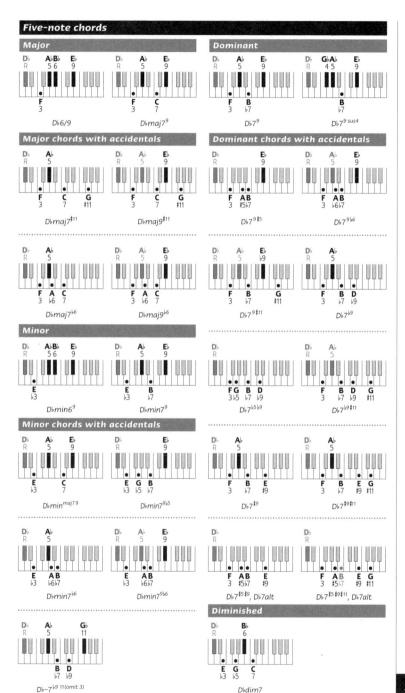

## Five-note chords

### Major

D♭6/9

D♭maj7⁹

### Major chords with accidentals

D♭maj7♯11

D♭maj9♯11

D♭maj7♭6

D♭maj9♭6

### Minor

D♭min6⁹

D♭min7⁹

### Minor chords with accidentals

D♭min^maj7 9

D♭min7♭9♭5

D♭min7♭6

D♭min7⁹♭6

D♭−7♭9 11(omit 3)

### Dominant

D♭7⁹

D♭7⁹ sus4

### Dominant chords with accidentals

D♭7⁹♯5

D♭7⁹♭6

D♭7⁹♯11

D♭7♭9

D♭7♭5♭9

D♭7♭9♯11

D♭7♯9

D♭7♯9♯11

D♭7♯5♯9, D♭7alt

D♭7♯5♯9♯11, D♭7alt

### Diminished

D♭dim7

---

*Enharmonic: C♯*

● ▌ Play these keys.

● ▌ Can be left out.

| | |
|---|---|
| ♭9 = ♭2 | |
| 9 = 2 | |
| ♯9 = ♭10 | |
| 11 = 4 | |
| ♯11 = ♯4 | |
| ♯11 = ♭5 | |
| ♭13 = ♯5 | |
| 13 = 6 | |
| ♭13 = ♭6 | |

**193**

# D

**Inversions**

**Three-note chords**

Root position:
R–3–5

First inversion:
3–5–R

Second inversion:
5–R–3

**Four-note chords**

Root position:
R–3–5–7

First inversion:
3–5–7–R

Second inversion:
5–7–R–3

Third inversion:
7–R–3–5

## Three-note chords

### Major

D

Dsus4

### Major with ♯ or ♭

D♭5

### Minor

Dmin

### Diminished

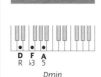

Ddim

## Four-note chords

### Major

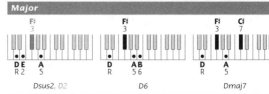

Dsus2, D2     D6     Dmaj7

### Major chords with accidentals

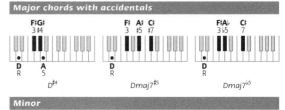

D♯4     Dmaj7♯5     Dmaj7♭5

### Minor

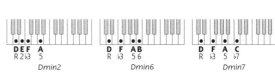

Dmin2     Dmin6     Dmin7

### Minor chords with accidentals

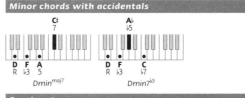

Daug     Dmin^maj7     Dmin7♭5

### Dominant

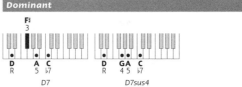

D7     D7sus4

### Dominant chords with accidentals

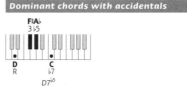

D7♭5

### Diminished

Ddim

194

# D

## Five-note chords

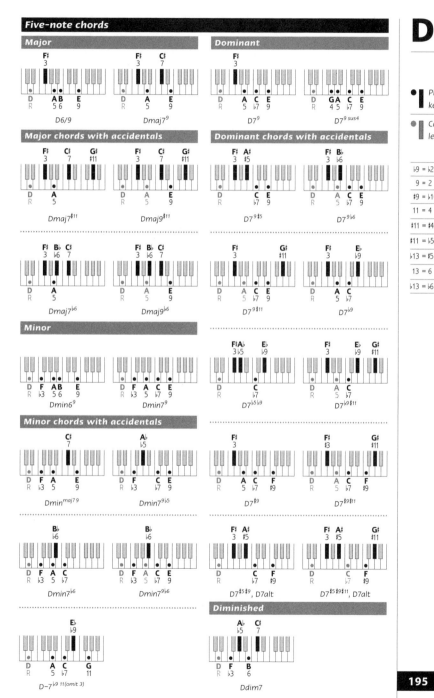

### Major

D6/9

Dmaj7⁹

### Major chords with accidentals

Dmaj7♯11

Dmaj9♯11

Dmaj7♭6

Dmaj9♭6

### Minor

Dmin6⁹

Dmin7⁹

### Minor chords with accidentals

Dmin^maj7 9

Dmin7⁹♭5

Dmin7♭6

Dmin7⁹♭6

D−7♭9 11(omit 3)

### Dominant

D7⁹

D7⁹ sus4

### Dominant chords with accidentals

D7⁹♯5

D7⁹♭6

D7⁹♯11

D7♭9

D7♭5♭9

D7♭9♯11

D7♯9

D7♯9♯11

D7♯5♯9, D7alt

D7♯5♯9♯11, D7alt

### Diminished

Ddim7

• | Play these keys.

• | Can be left out.

| | |
|---|---|
| ♭9 | ♭2 |
| 9 | 2 |
| ♯9 | ♭10 |
| 11 | 4 |
| ♯11 | ♯4 |
| ♯11 | ♭5 |
| ♭13 | ♯5 |
| 13 | 6 |
| ♭13 | ♭6 |

**195**

# E♭

*Enharmonic: D♯*

## Inversions

**Three-note chords**

Root position:
R–3–5

First inversion:
3–5–R

Second inversion:
5–R–3

**Four-note chords**

Root position:
R–3–5–7

First inversion:
3–5–7–R

Second inversion:
5–7–R–3

Third inversion:
7–R–3–5

## Three-note chords

### Major

E♭ B♭
R 5
G
3

E♭

### Major

A♭ B♭
4 5
E♭
R

E♭sus4

### Major with ♯ or ♭

E♭
R
G A
3 ♯5

E♭♭5

E♭
R
G B
3 ♯5

E♭aug

### Minor

E♭ G♭ B♭
R ♭3 5

E♭min

### Diminished

E♭ G♭
R ♭3
A
♭5

E♭dim

## Four-note chords

### Major

E♭ B♭
R 5
F G
2 3

E♭sus2, E♭2

E♭ B♭
R 5
G C
3 6

E♭6

E♭ B♭
R 5
G D
3 7

E♭maj7

### Major chords with accidentals

E♭ B♭
R 5
G A
3 ♯4

E♭♯4

E♭
R
G B D
3 ♯5 7

E♭maj7♯5

E♭
R
G A D
3 ♭5 7

E♭maj7♭5

### Minor

E♭ G♭ B♭
R ♭3 5
F
2

E♭min2

E♭ G♭ B♭
R ♭3 5
C
6

E♭min6

E♭ G♭ B♭ D♭
R ♭3 5 ♭7

E♭min7

### Minor chords with accidentals

E♭ G♭ B♭
R ♭3 5
D
7

E♭min^maj7

E♭ G♭ D♭
R ♭3 ♭7
A
♭5

E♭min7♭5

### Dominant

E♭ B♭ D♭
R 5 ♭7
G
3

E♭7

E♭ A♭ B♭ D♭
R 4 5 ♭7

E♭7sus4

### Dominant chords with accidentals

E♭ D♭
R ♭7
G A
3 ♭5

E♭♭5

### Diminished

E♭ G♭
R ♭3
A C
♭5 6

E♭dim

# Eb

Enharmonic: D#

## Five-note chords

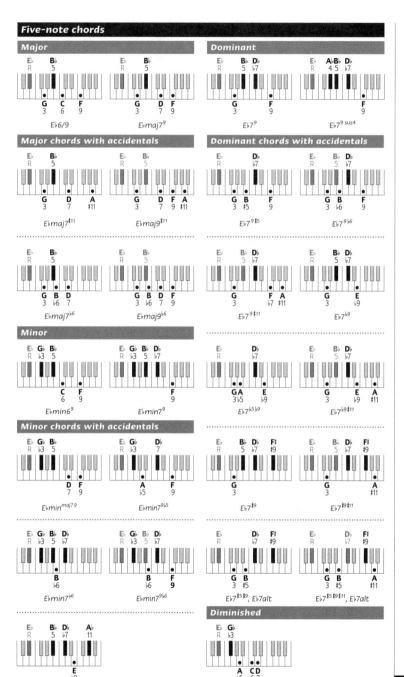

### Major

Eb6/9

Ebmaj7⁹

### Major chords with accidentals

Ebmaj7#11

Ebmaj9#11

Ebmaj7b6

Ebmaj9b6

### Minor

Ebmin6⁹

Ebmin7⁹

### Minor chords with accidentals

Ebminmaj79

Ebmin79b5

Ebmin7b6

Ebmin79b6

Eb-7b9 11(omit 3)

### Dominant

Eb7⁹

Eb7⁹ sus4

### Dominant chords with accidentals

Eb7⁹#5

Eb7⁹b6

Eb7⁹#11

Eb7b9

Eb7b5b9

Eb7b9#11

Eb7#9

Eb7#9#11

Eb7#5#9, Eb7alt

Eb7#5#9#11, Eb7alt

### Diminished

Ebdim7, Eb°7

● Play these keys.

● Can be left out.

| b9 = b2 |
| 9 = 2 |
| #9 = b10 |
| 11 = 4 |
| #11 = #4 |
| #11 = b5 |
| b13 = #5 |
| 13 = 6 |
| b13 = b6 |

# E

## Inversions

### Three-note chords

Root position:

R–3–5

First inversion:

3–5–R

Second inversion:

5–R–3

### Four-note chords

Root position:

R–3–5–7

First inversion:

3–5–7–R

Second inversion:

5–7–R–3

Third inversion:

7–R–3–5

### Three-note chords

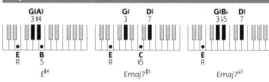

**Major**

E

Esus4

**Major with ♯ or ♭**

E♭5

Eaug

**Minor**

Emin

**Diminished**

Edim

### Four-note chords

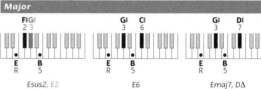

**Major**

Esus2, E2 • E6 • Emaj7, DΔ

**Major chords with accidentals**

E♯4 • Emaj7♯5 • Emaj7♭5

**Minor**

Emin2 • Emin6 • Emin7

**Minor chords with accidentals**

Emin^maj7 • Emin7♭5

**Dominant**

E7 • E7sus4

**Dominant chords with accidentals**

E7♭5

**Diminished**

Edim

## Five-note chords

**E**

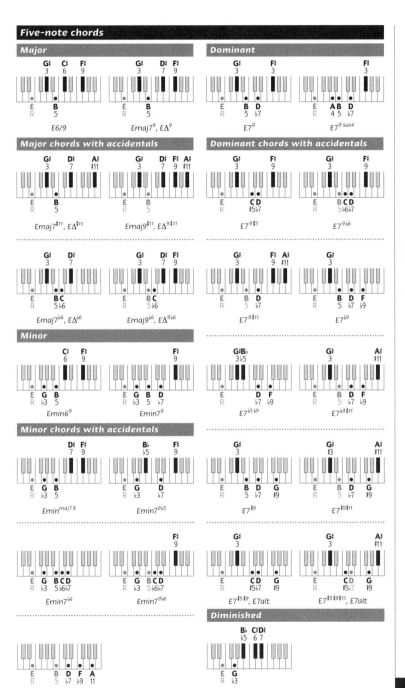

### Major

| G# | C# | F# |
| 3 | 6 | 9 |

E   B
R   5

E6/9

| G# | D# | F# |
| 3 | 7 | 9 |

E   B
R   5

Emaj7⁹, EΔ⁹

### Dominant

| G# | | F# |
| 3 | | 3 |

E   B  D
R   5  ♭7

E7⁹

| | | F# |
| | | 3 |

E   A B  D
R   4 5  ♭7

E7⁹ sus4

### Major chords with accidentals

| G# | D# | A# |
| 3 | 7 | #11 |

E   B
R   5

Emaj7#11, EΔ#11

| G# | D# | F# | A# |
| 3 | 7 | 9 | #11 |

E   B
R   5

Emaj9#11, EΔ9#11

### Dominant chords with accidentals

| G# | | F# |
| 3 | | 9 |

E   C D
R   #5 ♭7

E7⁹#5

| G# | | F# |
| 3 | | 9 |

E   B C D
R   5 ♭6 ♭7

E7⁹♭6

| G# | D# |
| 3 | 7 |

E   B C
R   5 ♭6

Emaj7♭6, EΔ♭6

| G# | D# | F# |
| 3 | 7 | 9 |

E   B C
R   5 ♭6

Emaj9♭6, EΔ9♭6

| G# | | F# | A# |
| 3 | | 9 | #11 |

E   B  D
R   5  ♭7

E7⁹#11

| G# | |
| 3 | |

E   B  D  F
R   5  ♭7 ♭9

E7♭9

### Minor

| C# | F# |
| 6 | 9 |

E   G  B
R   ♭3 5

Emin6⁹

| | F# |
| | 9 |

E   G  B  D
R   ♭3 5  7

Emin7⁹

| G#B♭ | |
| 3♭5 | |

E   D  F
R   ♭7 ♭9

E7♭5♭9

| G# | | A# |
| 3 | | #11 |

E   B  D  F
R   5  ♭7 ♭9

E7♭9#11

### Minor chords with accidentals

| D# | F# |
| 7 | 9 |

E   G  B
R   ♭3 5

Emin maj7 9

| B♭ | F# |
| ♭5 | 9 |

E   G  D
R   ♭3  ♭7

Emin7⁹♭5

| G# | |
| 3 | |

E   B  D
R   5  ♭7

E7#9

| G# | | A# |
| #3 | | #11 |

E   B  D  G
R   5  ♭7 #9

E7#9#11

| | F# |
| | 9 |

E   G  B C D
R   ♭3 5 ♭6♭7

Emin7♭6

| | F# |
| | 9 |

E   G  B C D
R   ♭3 5 ♭6♭7

Emin7⁹♭6

| G# | |
| 3 | |

E   C D  G
R   #5♭7 #9

E7#5#9, E7alt

| G# | | A# |
| 3 | | #11 |

E   C D  G
R   #5♭7 #9

E7#5#9#11, E7alt

E   B  D  F  A
R   5  ♭7 ♭9 11

E-7♭9 11(omit 3)

### Diminished

| B♭ | C#D# |
| ♭5 | 6 7 |

E   G
R   ♭3

Edim7

# F

**Inversions**

**Three-note chords**

Root position:
R–3–5

First inversion:
3–5–R

Second inversion:
5–R–3

**Four-note chords**

Root position:
R–3–5–7

First inversion:
3–5–7–R

Second inversion:
5–7–R–3

Third inversion:
7–R–3–5

**Three-note chords**

## Three-note chords

### Major

F A C
R 3 5

F

B♭
4

F C
R 5

Fsus4

### Major with ♯ or ♭

F A B
R R♭5

F♭5

C♯
♯5

F A
R 3

Faug

### Minor

A♭
♭3

F C
R 5

Fmin

### Diminished

A♭
♭3

F B
R ♭5

Fdim

## Four-note chords

### Major

F G A   C
R 2 3   5

Fsus2, F2

F A C D
R 3 5 6

F6

F A C E
R 3 5 7

Fmaj7

### Major chords with accidentals

F A B C
R 3 ♯4 5

F♯4

C♯
♯5

F A E
R 3 7

Fmaj7♯5

F A B E
R 3♭5 7

Fmaj7♭5

### Minor

A♭
♭3

F G C
R 2 5

Fmin2

A♭
♭3

F C D
R 5 6

Fmin6

A♭  E♭
♭3  ♭7

F C
R 5

Fmin7

### Minor chords with accidentals

A♭
♭3

F C E
R 5 7

Fmin^maj7

A♭  E♭
♭3  ♭7

F B
R ♭7

Fmin7♭5

### Dominant

E♭
♭7

F A C
R 5 5

F7

B♭  E♭
4   ♭7

F C
R 5

F7sus4

### Dominant chords with accidentals

E♭
♭7

F A B
R 3♭5

F7♭5

### Diminished

A♭
♭3

F B D
R ♭5 6

Fdim

## Five-note chords

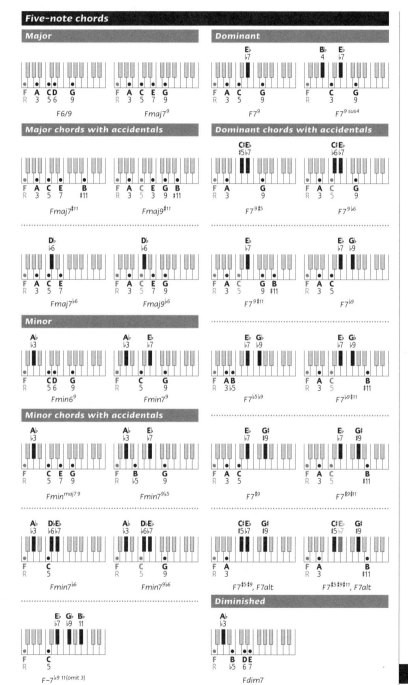

### Major

F6/9
Fmaj7⁹

### Major chords with accidentals

Fmaj7♯11
Fmaj9♯11

Fmaj7♭6
Fmaj9♭6

### Minor

Fmin6⁹
Fmin7⁹

### Minor chords with accidentals

Fmin^maj7 9
Fmin7♭5

Fmin7♭6
Fmin7♭6

F–7♭9 11(omit 3)

### Dominant

F7⁹
F7⁹ sus4

### Dominant chords with accidentals

F7⁹♯5
F7♭6

F7⁹♯11
F7♭9

F7♭5♭9
F7♭9♯11

F7♯9
F7♯9♯11

F7♯5♯9, F7alt
F7♯5♯9♯11, F7alt

### Diminished

Fdim7

**F**

● ▌ Play these
 ▌ keys.

● ▌ Can be
 ▌ left out.

| ♭9 = ♭2 |
| 9 = 2 |
| ♯9 = ♭10 |
| 11 = 4 |
| ♯11 = ♯4 |
| ♯11 = ♭5 |
| ♭13 = ♯5 |
| 13 = 6 |
| ♭13 = ♭6 |

# F#

*Enharmonic:* G♭

**Inversions**

***Three-note chords***

Root position:
R-3-5

First inversion:
3-5-R

Second inversion:
5-R-3

***Four-note chords***

Root position:
R-3-5-7

First inversion:
3-5-7-R

Second inversion:
5-7-R-3

Third inversion:
7-R-3-5

**Three-note chords**

**Major**

F#

F#sus4

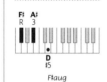

F#♭5

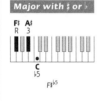

F#aug

**Minor**

F#min

**Diminished**

F#dim

**Four-note chords**

**Major**

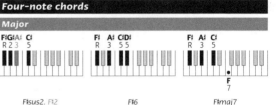

F#sus2, F#2      F#6      F#maj7

**Major chords with accidentals**

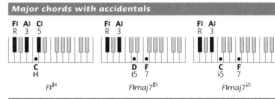

F#♯4      F#maj7♯5      F#maj7♭5

**Minor**

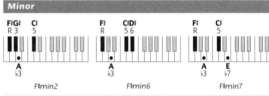

F#min2      F#min6      F#min7

**Minor chords with accidentals**

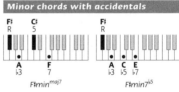

F#min^maj7      F#min7♭5

**Dominant**

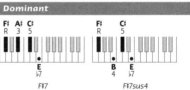

F#7      F#7sus4

**Dominant chords with accidentals**

F#7♭5

**Diminished**

F#dim

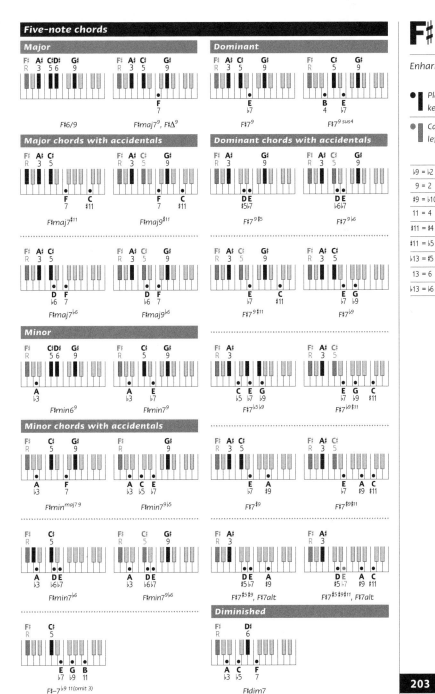

# Five-note chords

## Major

F#6/9

F#maj7⁹, F#Δ⁹

## Major chords with accidentals

F#maj7#11

F#maj9#11

F#maj7♭6

F#maj9♭6

## Minor

F#min6⁹

F#min7⁹

## Minor chords with accidentals

F#min^maj7 9

F#min7⁹♭5

F#min7♭6

F#min7⁹♭6

F#–7♭9 11(omit 3)

## Dominant

F#7⁹

F#7⁹ sus4

## Dominant chords with accidentals

F#7⁹#5

F#7⁹♭6

F#7⁹#11

F#7♭9

F#7♭5♭9

F#7♭9#11

F#7#9

F#7♭9#11

F#7#5♭9, F#7alt

F#7#5♭9#11, F#7alt

## Diminished

F#dim7

**Enharmonic: G♭**

● ❙ Play these keys.

● ❙ Can be left out.

| ♭9 | = | ♭2 |
|---|---|---|
| 9 | = | 2 |
| #9 | = | ♭10 |
| 11 | = | 4 |
| #11 | = | #4 |
| #11 | = | ♭5 |
| ♭13 | = | #5 |
| 13 | = | 6 |
| ♭13 | = | ♭6 |

**203**

**TIPBOOK KEYBOARD AND DIGITAL PIANO**



# G

**Inversions**

**Three-note chords**

Root position:
R–3–5

First inversion:
3–5–R

Second inversion:
5–R–3

**Four-note chords**

Root position:
R–3–5–7

First inversion:
3–5–7–R

Second inversion:
5–7–R–3

Third inversion:
7–R–3–5

## Three-note chords

### Major

G
R

B
3

D
5

*G*

### Major with ♯ or ♭

D♭
♭5

G
R

B
3

*G♭5*

D♯
♯5

G
R

B
3

*Gaug*

### Minor

B♭
♭3

G
R

D
5

*Gmin*

### Diminished

B♭
♭3

D♭
♭5

G
R

*Gdim*

## Four-note chords

### Major

G A B
R 2 3

D
5

*Gsus2, G2*

G
R

B
3

D E
5 6

*G6*

F♯
7

G
R

B
3

D
5

*Gmaj7*

### Major chords with accidentals

C♯
♯4

G
R

C D
4 5

*Gsus4*

D♯ F♯
♯5 7

G
R

B
3

D
5

*G♯4*

D♭ F♯
♭5 7

G
R

B
3

*Gmaj7♯5*

G
R

B
3

*Gmaj7♭5*

### Minor

B♭
♭3

G A
R 2

D
5

*Gmin2*

B♭
♭3

G
R

D E
5 6

*Gmin6*

B♭
♭3

G
R

D F
5 ♭7

*Gmin7*

### Minor chords with accidentals

D♯
♯5

G
R

B
3

*Gaug*

B♭ F♯
♭3 7

G
R

D
5

*Gmin^maj7*

B♭ D♭
♭3 ♭5

G
R

F
♭7

*Gmin7♭5*

### Dominant

G
R

B
3

D F
5 ♭7

*G7*

G
R

C D
4 5

F
♭7

*G7sus4*

### Dominant chords with accidentals

D♭
♭5

G
R

B
3

F
♭7

*G7♭5*

### Diminished

B♭ D♭
♭3 ♭5

G
R

E
6

*Gdim*



**204**

# G

## Five-note chords

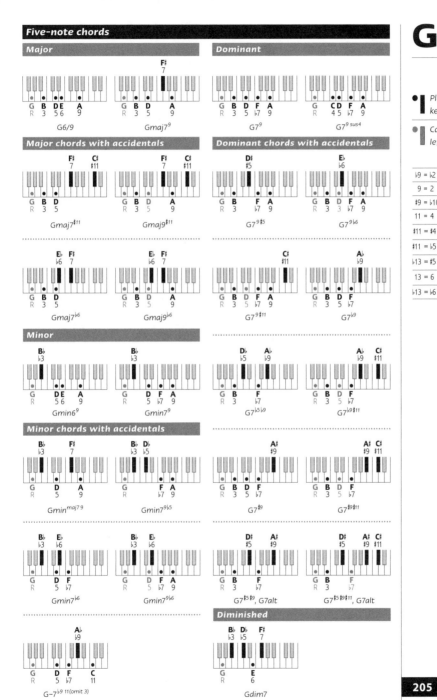

### Major

G6/9

Gmaj7⁹

### Major chords with accidentals

Gmaj7♯11

Gmaj9♯11

Gmaj7♭6

Gmaj9♭6

### Minor

Gmin6⁹

Gmin7⁹

### Minor chords with accidentals

Gmin^maj7 9

Gmin7⁹♭5

Gmin7♭6

Gmin7⁹♭6

G−7♭9 11(omit 3)

### Dominant

G7⁹

G7⁹ sus4

### Dominant chords with accidentals

G7⁹♯5

G7⁹♭6

G7⁹♯11

G7♭9

G7♭5♭9

G7♭9♯11

G7♯9

G7♯9♯11

G7♯5♯9, G7alt

G7♯5♯9♯11, G7alt

### Diminished

Gdim7

● ▌ Play these keys.

● ▌ Can be left out.

| ♭9 = ♭2 |
| 9 = 2 |
| ♯9 = ♭10 |
| 11 = 4 |
| ♯11 = ♯4 |
| ♯11 = ♭5 |
| ♭13 = ♯5 |
| 13 = 6 |
| ♭13 = ♭6 |

**205**

**A♭**

Enharmonic: G♯

**Inversions**

**Three-note chords**

Root position:
R–3–5

First inversion:
3–5–R

Second inversion:
5–R–3

**Four-note chords**

Root position:
R–3–5–7

First inversion:
3–5–7–R

Second inversion:
5–7–R–3

Third inversion:
7–R–3–5

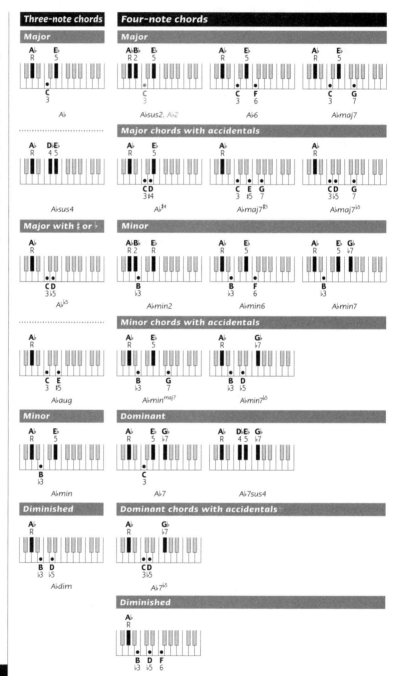

# Five-note chords

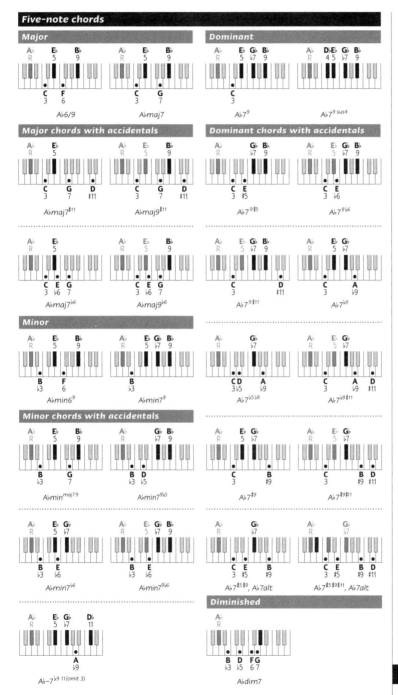

## Major

A♭ E♭ B♭
R 5 9
C F
3 6
A♭6/9

A♭ E♭ B♭
R 5 9
C G
3 7
A♭maj7

## Major chords with accidentals

A♭ E♭
R 5
C G D
3 7 ♯11
A♭maj7♯11

A♭ E♭ B♭
R 5 9
C G D
3 7 ♯11
A♭maj9♯11

A♭ E♭
R 5
C E G
3 ♭6 7
A♭maj7♭6

A♭ E♭ B♭
R 5 9
C E G
3 ♭6 7
A♭maj9♭6

## Minor

A♭ E♭ B♭
R 5 9
B F
♭3 6
A♭min6⁹

A♭ E♭ G♭ B♭
R 5 ♭7 9
B
♭3
A♭min7⁹

## Minor chords with accidentals

A♭ E♭ B♭
R 5 9
B G
♭3 7
A♭min^maj79

A♭ G♭ B♭
R ♭7 9
B D
♭3 ♭5
A♭min7⁹♭5

A♭ E♭ G♭
R 5 ♭7
B E
♭3 6
A♭min7♭6

A♭ E♭ G♭ B♭
R 5 ♭7 9
B E
♭3 6
A♭min7⁹♭6

A♭ E♭ G♭ D♭
R 5 ♭7 11
A
♭9
A♭−7♭9 11(omit 3)

## Dominant

A♭ E♭ G♭ B♭
R 5 ♭7 9
C
3
A♭7⁹

A♭ D♭E♭ G♭ B♭
R 4 5 ♭7 9
C
3
A♭7⁹ sus4

## Dominant chords with accidentals

A♭ G♭ B♭
R ♭7 9
C E
3 ♯5
A♭7⁹♯5

A♭ E♭ G♭ B♭
R 5 ♭7 9
C E
3 ♭6
A♭7⁹♭6

A♭ E♭ G♭ B♭
R 5 ♭7 9
C D
3 ♯11
A♭7⁹♯11

A♭ E♭ G♭
R 5 ♭7
C A
3 ♭9
A♭7♭9

A♭ G♭
R ♭7
C D A
3 ♯5 ♭9
A♭7♭5♭9

A♭ E♭ G♭
R 5 ♭7
C A D
3 ♭9 ♯11
A♭7♭9♯11

A♭ E♭ G♭
R 5 ♭7
C B
3 ♯9
A♭7♯9

A♭ E♭ G♭
R 5 ♭7
C B D
3 ♯9 ♯11
A♭7♯9♯11

A♭ G♭
R ♭7
C E B
3 ♯5 ♯9
A♭7♯5♯9, A♭7alt

A♭ G♭
R ♭7
C E B D
3 ♯5 ♯9 ♯11
A♭7♯5♯9♯11, A♭7alt

## Diminished

A♭
R
B D FG
♭3 ♭5 6 7
A♭dim7

# A♭

Enharmonic: G♯

● | Play these keys.

● | Can be left out.

| ♭9 = ♭2 |
| 9 = 2 |
| ♯9 = ♭10 |
| 11 = 4 |
| ♯11 = ♯4 |
| ♯11 = ♭5 |
| ♭13 = ♯5 |
| 13 = 6 |
| ♭13 = ♭6 |

207

# A

**Inversions**

**Three-note chords**

Root position:
R-3-5

First inversion:
3-5-R

Second inversion:
5-R-3

**Four-note chords**

Root position:
R-3-5-7

First inversion:
3-5-7-R

Second inversion:
5-7-R-3

Third inversion:
7-R-3-5

| Three-note chords | Four-note chords |
|---|---|

## Major

A
R ... 5
E

A

## Major

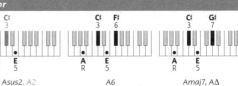

AB E
R 2 ... 5

Asus2, A2

A6

Amaj7, A∆

## Major chords with accidentals

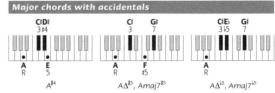

A D E
R ... 4 5

Asus4

A♯4

A∆♯5, Amaj7♯5

A∆♭5, Amaj7♭5

## Major with ♯ or ♭

A
R

A♭5

A+, Aaug

## Minor

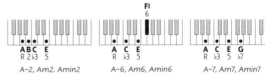

ABC E
R 2♭3 5

A-2, Am2. Amin2

A-6, Am6, Amin6

A-7, Am7, Amin7

## Minor chords with accidentals

A C E
R ♭3 5

A-△7, Am△7, Amin^maj7

Am7♭5, Aø, A-7♭5, Amin7♭5

## Minor

A C E
R ♭3 5

A-, Amin, Am

## Dominant

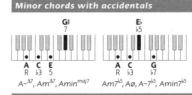

A E G
R 5 ♭7

A7

A DE G
R 45 ♭7

A7sus4

## Diminished

A C
R ♭3

Adim, A°

## Dominant chords with accidentals

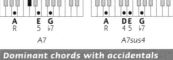

A G
R ♭7

A7♭5

## Diminished

A C
R ♭3

Adim, A°

## Five-note chords

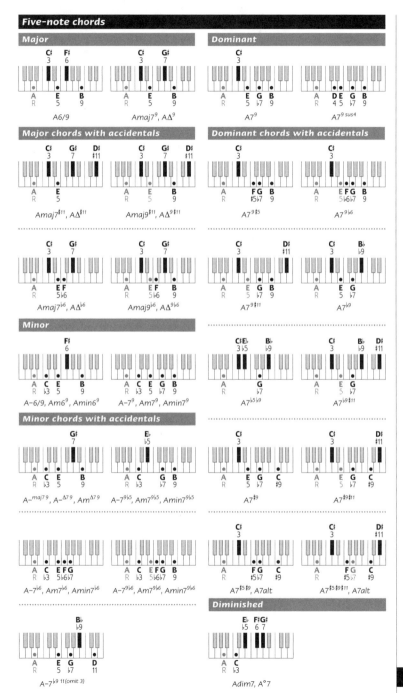

### Major

**C♯ F♯**
3 6

A6/9
A E B
R 5 9

**C♯ G♯**
3 7

Amaj7⁹, AΔ⁹
A E B
R 5 9

### Dominant

**C♯**
3

A7⁹
A E G B
R 5 ♭7 9

**C♯**
3

A7⁹ˢᵘˢ⁴
A DE G B
R 4 5 ♭7 9

### Major chords with accidentals

**C♯ G♯ D♯**
3 7 ♯11

Amaj7♯¹¹, AΔ♯¹¹
A E
R 5

**C♯ G♯ D♯**
3 7 ♯11

Amaj9♯¹¹, AΔ⁹♯¹¹
A E B
R 5 9

### Dominant chords with accidentals

**C♯**
3

A7⁹♯⁵
A FG B
R ♯5♭7 9

**C♯**
3

A7⁹♭⁶
A EFG B
R 5♭6♭7 9

**C♯ G♯**
3 7

Amaj7♭⁶, AΔ♭⁶
A EF
R 5♭6

**C♯ G♯**
3 7

Amaj9♭⁶, AΔ⁹♭⁶
A EF B
R 5♭6 9

**C♯ D♯**
3 ♯11

A7⁹♯¹¹
A E G B
R 5 ♭7 9

**C♯ B♭**
3 ♭9

A7♭⁹
A E G
R 5 ♭7

### Minor

**F♯**
6

A–6/9, Am6⁹, Amin6⁹
A C E B
R ♭3 5 9

A–7⁹, Am7⁹, Amin7⁹
A C E G B
R ♭3 5 ♭7 9

**C♯E♭ B♭**
3♭5 ♭9

A7♭⁵♭⁹
A G
R ♭7

**C♯ B♭ D♯**
3 ♭9 ♯11

A7♭⁹♯¹¹
A E G
R 5 ♭7

### Minor chords with accidentals

**G♯**
7

A–ᵐᵃʲ⁷⁹, A–Δ⁷⁹, Amᐃ⁷⁹
A C E B
R ♭3 5 9

**E♭**
♭5

A–7♭⁹♭⁵, Am7⁹♭⁵, Amin7⁹♭⁵
A C G B
R ♭3 ♭7 9

**C♯**
3

A7♯⁹
A E G C
R 5 ♭7 ♯9

**C♯ D♯**
3 ♯11

A7♯⁹♯¹¹
A E G C
R 5 ♭7 ♯9

A–7♭⁶, Am7♭⁶, Amin7♭⁶
A C EFG
R ♭3 5♭6♭7

A–7⁹♭⁶, Am7⁹♭⁶, Amin7⁹♭⁶
A C EFG B
R ♭3 5♭6♭7 9

**C♯**
3

A7♯⁵♯⁹, A7alt
A FG C
R ♯5♭7 ♯9

**C♯ D♯**
3 ♯11

A7♯⁵♯⁹♯¹¹, A7alt
A FG C
R ♯5♭7 ♯9

**B♭**
♭9

A–7♭⁹¹¹(omit 3)
A E G D
R 5 ♭7 11

### Diminished

**E♭ F♯G♯**
♭5 6 7

Adim7, A°7
A C
R ♭3

**A**

● ▌ Play these keys.

● ▌ Can be left out.

| | |
|---|---|
| ♭9 = ♭2 | |
| 9 = 2 | |
| ♯9 = ♭10 | |
| 11 = 4 | |
| ♯11 = ♯4 | |
| ♯11 = ♭5 | |
| ♭13 = ♯5 | |
| 13 = 6 | |
| ♭13 = ♭6 | |

# B♭

*Enharmonic: A♯*

**Inversions**

**Three-note chords**

Root position:
R–3–5

First inversion:
3–5–R

Second inversion:
5–R–3

**Four-note chords**

Root position:
R–3–5–7

First inversion:
3–5–7–R

Second inversion:
5–7–R–3

Third inversion:
7–R–3–5

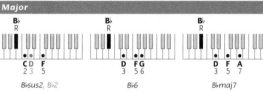

## Three-note chords

### Major

B♭

B♭sus4

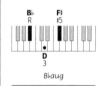

### Major with ♯ or ♭

B♭♭5

B♭aug

### Minor

B♭min

### Diminished

B♭dim

## Four-note chords

### Major

B♭6     B♭maj7

B♭sus2, B♭2

### Major chords with accidentals

B♭♯4    B♭maj7♯5    B♭maj7♭5

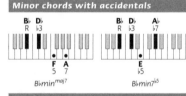

### Minor

B♭min2    B♭min6    B♭min7

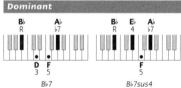

### Minor chords with accidentals

B♭min^maj7    B♭min7♭5

### Dominant

B♭7     B♭7sus4

### Dominant chords with accidentals

B♭7♭5

### Diminished

B♭dim

## Five-note chords

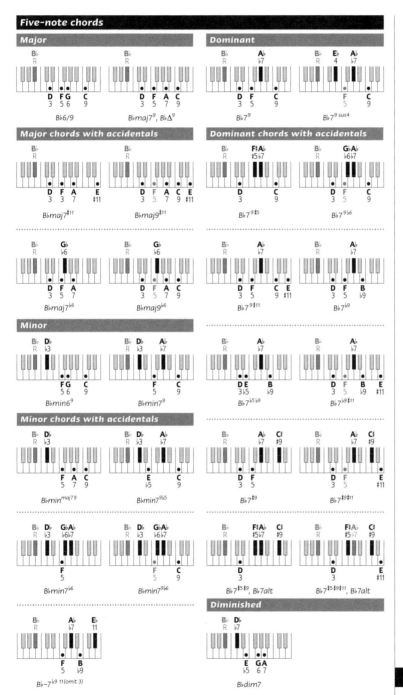

### Major

Bb6/9

Bbmaj7⁹, BbΔ⁹

### Major chords with accidentals

Bbmaj7#11

Bbmaj9#11

Bbmaj7b6

Bbmaj9b6

### Minor

Bbmin6⁹

Bbmin7⁹

### Minor chords with accidentals

Bbmin^maj79

Bbmin7b5

Bbmin7b6

Bbmin7⁹b6

Bb-7b9 11(omit 3)

### Dominant

Bb7⁹

Bb7⁹ sus4

### Dominant chords with accidentals

Bb7⁹#5

Bb7⁹b6

Bb7⁹#11

Bb7b9

Bb7b5 b9

Bb7b9#11

Bb7#9

Bb7#9#11

Bb7#5#9, Bb7alt

Bb7#5#9#11, Bb7alt

### Diminished

Bbdim7

**Bb**

Enharmonic: A#

● Play these keys.

● Can be left out.

| | |
|---|---|
| b9 = b2 | |
| 9 = 2 | |
| #9 = b10 | |
| 11 = 4 | |
| #11 = #4 | |
| #11 = b5 | |
| b13 = #5 | |
| 13 = 6 | |
| b13 = b6 | |

# B

**Inversions**

**Three-note chords**

Root position:
R–3–5

First inversion:
3–5–R

Second inversion:
5–R–3

**Four-note chords**

Root position:
R–3–5–7

First inversion:
3–5–7–R

Second inversion:
5–7–R–3

Third inversion:
7–R–3–5

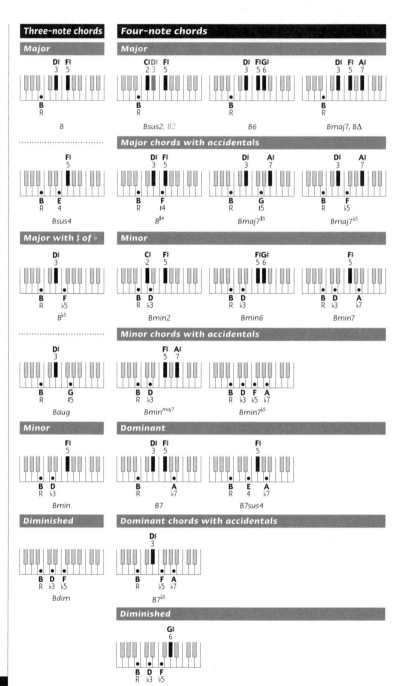

## Five-note chords

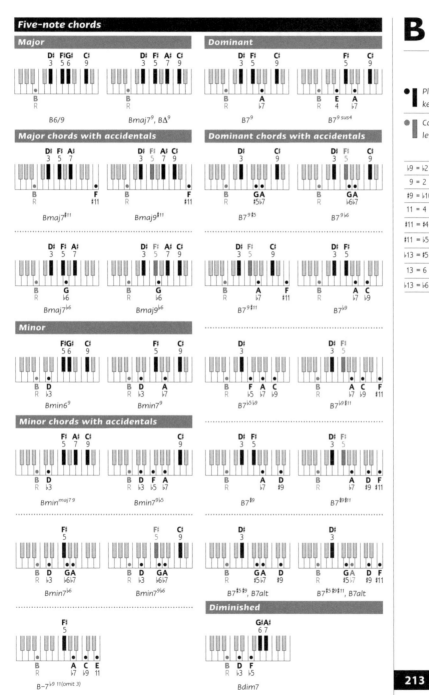

### Major

**D♯ F♯G♯ C♯**
3 5 6 9

**B**
R

B6/9

**D♯ F♯ A♯ C♯**
3 5 7 9

**B**
R

Bmaj7⁹, BΔ⁹

### Dominant

**D♯ F♯ C♯**
3 5 9

**B** **A**
R ♭7

B7⁹

**F♯ C♯**
5 9

**B** **E** **A**
R 4 ♭7

B7⁹ ˢᵘˢ⁴

### Major chords with accidentals

**D♯ F♯ A♯**
3 5 7

**B** **F**
R ♯11

Bmaj7♯¹¹

**D♯ F♯ A♯ C♯**
3 5 7 9

**B** **F**
R ♯11

Bmaj9♯¹¹

**D♯ F♯ A♯**
3 5 7

**B** **G**
R ♭6

Bmaj7♭⁶

**D♯ F♯ A♯ C♯**
3 5 7 9

**B** **G**
R ♭6

Bmaj9♭⁶

### Dominant chords with accidentals

**D♯**
3

**C♯**
9

**B** **GA**
R ♯5♭7

B7⁹♯⁵

**D♯ F♯**
3 5

**C♯**
9

**B** **GA**
R ♭6♭7

B7⁹♭⁶

**D♯ F♯**
3 5

**C♯**
9

**B** **A** **F**
R ♭7 ♯11

B7⁹♯¹¹

**D♯ F♯**
3 5

**B** **A** **C**
R ♭7 ♭9

B7♭⁹

### Minor

**F♯G♯ C♯**
5 6 9

**B** **D**
R ♭3

Bmin6⁹

**F♯ C♯**
5 9

**B** **D** **A**
R ♭3 ♭7

Bmin7⁹

**D♯**
3

**B** **F** **A** **C**
R ♭5 ♭7 ♭9

B7♭⁵♭⁹

**D♯ F♯**
3 5

**B** **A** **C** **F**
R ♭7 ♭9 ♯11

B7♭⁹♯¹¹

### Minor chords with accidentals

**F♯ A♯ C♯**
5 7 9

**B** **D**
R ♭3

Bmin^maj7 9

**C♯**
9

**B** **D** **F** **A**
R ♭3 ♭5 ♭7

Bmin7⁹♭⁵

**D♯ F♯**
3 5

**B** **A** **D**
R ♭7 ♯9

B7♯⁹

**D♯ F♯**
3 5

**B** **A** **D** **F**
R ♭7 ♯9 ♯11

B7♯⁹♯¹¹

**F♯**
5

**B** **D** **GA**
R ♭3 ♭6♭7

Bmin7♭⁶

**F♯ C♯**
5 9

**B** **D** **GA**
R ♭3 ♭6♭7

Bmin7⁹♭⁶

**D♯**
3

**B** **GA** **D**
R ♯5♭7 ♯9

B7♯⁵♯⁹, B7alt

**D♯**
3

**B** **GA** **D** **F**
R ♯5♭7 ♯9 ♯11

B7♯⁵♯⁹♯¹¹, B7alt

**F♯**
5

**B** **A** **C** **E**
R ♭7 ♭9 11

B–7♭⁹ ¹¹⁽ᵒᵐⁱᵗ ³⁾

### Diminished

**G♯A♯**
6 7

**B** **D** **F**
R ♭3 ♭5

Bdim7

# B

● **▮** Play these keys.

● **▮** Can be left out.

| | |
|---|---|
| ♭9 | = ♭2 |
| 9 | = 2 |
| ♯9 | = ♭10 |
| 11 | = 4 |
| ♯11 | = ♯4 |
| ♯11 | = ♭5 |
| ♭13 | = ♯5 |
| 13 | = 6 |
| ♭13 | = ♭6 |

**213**

# Essential Data

*In the event of your equipment being stolen or lost, or if you decide to sell it, it's useful to have all relevant data at hand. You can make these essential notes on this page. For the insurance, for the police, or just for yourself.*

**INSURANCE**

Company:                                     Phone:

Broker:                                      Phone:

Email:                                       Website:

Policy number:                               Premium:

Renewal date:

**INSTRUMENTS AND ACCESSORIES**

Make and model:

Serial number:

Price:                                       Date of purchase:

Dealer:                                      Phone:

E-mail:                                       Website:


Make and model:

Serial number:

Price:                                       Date of purchase:

Dealer:                                      Phone:

E-mail:                                       Website:


Make and model:

Serial number:

Price:                                       Date of purchase:

Dealer:                                      Phone:

E-mail:                                       Website:

Make and model:

Serial number:

Price:                              Date of purchase:

Dealer:                            Phone:

E-mail:                            Website:

**ADDITIONAL NOTES**

# Index

Please check out the glossary on pages 165–171 for additional definitions of the terms used in this book.

**217**

# The Tipbook Series

*Did you like this Tipbook? There are also Tipbooks for your fellow band or orchestra members! The Tipbook Series features various books on musical instruments, including the singing voice, in addition to Tipbook Music on Paper, Tipbook Amplifiers and Effects, and Tipbook Music for Kids and Teens – a Guide for Parents.*

*Every Tipbook is a highly accessible and easy-to-read compilation of the knowledge and expertise of numerous musicians, teachers, technicians, and other experts, written for musicians of all ages, at all levels, and in any style of music. Please check www.tipbook.com for up to date information on the Tipbook Series!*

*All Tipbooks come with Tipcodes that offer additional information, sound files and short movies at www.tipbook.com*

### Instrument Tipbooks

All instrument Tipbooks offer a wealth of highly accessible, yet well-founded information on one or more closely related instruments. The first chapters of each Tipbook explain the very basics of the instrument(s), explaining all the parts and what they do, describing what's involved in learning to play, and indicating typical instrument prices. The core chapters, addressing advanced players as well, turn you into an instant expert on the instrument. This knowledge allows you to make an informed purchase and get the most out of your instrument. Comprehensive chapters on maintenance, intonation, and tuning are also included, as well a brief section on the history, the family, and the production of the instrument.

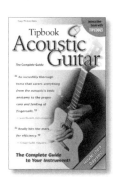

### Tipbook Acoustic Guitar – $14.95

*Tipbook Acoustic Guitar* explains all of the elements that allow you to recognize and judge a guitar's timbre, performance, and playability, focusing on both steel-string and nylon-string instruments. There are chapters covering the various types of strings and their characteristics, and there's plenty of helpful information on changing and cleaning strings, on tuning and maintenance, and even on the care of your fingernails.

**219**

### Tipbook Amplifiers and Effects – $14.99

Whether you need a guitar amp, a sound system, a multi-effects unit for a bass guitar, or a keyboard amplifier, *Tipbook Amplifiers and Effects* helps you to make a good choice. Two chapters explain general features (controls, equalizers, speakers, MIDI, etc.) and figures (watts, ohms, impedance, etc.), and further chapters cover the specifics of guitar amps, bass amps, keyboard amps, acoustic amps, and sound systems. Effects and effect units are dealt with in detail, and there are also chapters on microphones and pickups, and cables and wireless systems.

### Tipbook Cello – $14.95

Cellists can find everything they need to know about their instrument in *Tipbook Cello*. The book gives you tips on how to select an instrument and choose a bow, tells you all about the various types of strings and rosins, and gives you helpful tips on the maintenance and tuning of your instrument. Basic information on electric cellos is included as well!

### Tipbook Clarinet – $14.99

*Tipbook Clarinet* sheds light on every element of this fascinating instrument. The knowledge presented in this guide makes trying out and selecting a clarinet much easier, and it turns you into an instant expert on offset and in-line trill keys, rounded or French-style keys, and all other aspects of the instrument. Special chapters are devoted to reeds (selecting, testing, and adjusting reeds), mouthpieces and ligatures, and maintenance.

### Tipbook Electric Guitar and Bass Guitar – $14.95

Electric guitars and bass guitars come in many shapes and sizes. *Tipbook Electric Guitar and Bass Guitar* explains all of their features and characteristics, from neck profiles, frets, and types of wood to different types of pickups, tuning machines, and — of course — strings. Tuning and advanced do-it-yourself intonation techniques are included.

220

### Tipbook Drums – $14.95

A drum is a drum is a drum? Not true — and *Tipbook Drums* tells you all the ins and outs of their differences, from the type of wood to the dimensions of the shell, the shape of the bearing edge, and the drum's hardware. Special chapters discuss selecting drum sticks, drum heads, and cymbals. Tuning and muffling, two techniques a drummer must master to make the instrument sound as good as it can, are covered in detail, providing step-by-step instructions.

### Tipbook Flute and Piccolo – $14.99

Flute prices range from a few hundred to fifty thousand dollars and more. *Tipbook Flute and Piccolo* tells you how workmanship, materials, and other elements make for different instruments with vastly different prices, and teaches you how to find the instrument that best suits your or your child's needs. Open-hole or closed-hole keys, a B-foot or a C-foot, split-E or donut, inline or offset G? You'll be able to answer all these questions — and more — after reading this guide.

### Tipbook Keyboard and Digital Piano – $14.99

Buying a home keyboard or a digital piano may find you confronted with numerous unfamiliar terms. *Tipbook Keyboard and Digital Piano* explains all of them in a very easy-to-read fashion — from hammer action and non-weighted keys to MIDI, layers and splits, arpeggiators and sequencers, expression pedals and multi-switches, and more, including special chapters on how to judge the instrument's sound, accompaniment systems, and the various types of connections these instruments offer.

### Tipbook Music for Kids and Teens – a Guide for Parents – $14.99

How do you inspire children to play music? How do you inspire them to practice? What can you do to help them select an instrument, to reduce stage fright, or to practice effectively? What can you do to make practice fun? How do you reduce sound levels and

221

prevent hearing damage? These and many more questions are dealt with in *Tipbook Music for Kids and Teens – a Guide for Parents and Caregivers.* The book addresses all subjects related to the musical education of children from pre-birth to pre-adulthood.

### Tipbook Music on Paper – $14.99

*Tipbook Music on Paper – Basic Theory* offers everything you need to read and understand the language of music. The book presumes no prior understanding of theory and begins with the basics, explaining standard notation, but moves on to advanced topics such as odd time signatures and transposing music in a fashion that makes things really easy to understand.

### Tipbook Piano – $14.99

Choosing a piano becomes a lot easier with the knowledge provided in *Tipbook Piano*, which makes for a better understanding of this complex, expensive instrument without going into too much detail. How to judge and compare piano keyboards and pedals, the influence of the instrument's dimensions, different types of cabinets, how to judge an instrument's timbre, the difference between laminated and solid wood soundboards, accessories, hybrid and digital pianos, and why tuning and regulation are so important: Everything is covered in this handy guide.

### Tipbook Saxophone – $14.95

At first glance, all alto saxophones look alike. And all tenor saxophones do too — yet they all play and sound different from each other. *Tipbook Saxophone* discusses the instrument in detail, explaining the key system and the use of additional keys, the different types of pads, corks, and springs, mouthpieces and how they influence timbre and  playability, reeds (and how to select and adjust them) and much more. Fingering charts are also included!

222

### Tipbook Trumpet and Trombone, Flugelhorn and Cornet – $14.99

The Tipbook on brass instruments focuses on the smaller horns listed in the title. It explains all of the jargon you come across when you're out to buy or rent an instrument, from bell material to the shape of the bore, the leadpipe, valves and valve slides, and all other elements of the horn. Mouthpieces, a crucial choice for the sound and playability of all brasswinds, are covered in a separate chapter.

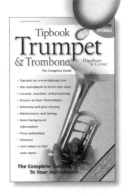

### Tipbook Violin and Viola – $14.95

*Tipbook Violin and Viola* covers a wide range of subjects, ranging from an explanation of different types of tuning pegs, fine tuners, and tailpieces, to how body dimensions and the bridge may influence the instrument's timbre. Tips on trying out instruments and bows are included. Special chapters are devoted to the characteristics of different types of strings, bows, and rosins, allowing you to get the most out of your instrument.

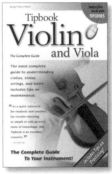

### Tipbook Vocals – The Singing Voice – $14.95

*Tipbook Vocals –The Singing Voice* helps you realize the full potential of your singing voice. The book, written in close collaboration with classical and non-classical singers and teachers, allows you to discover the world's most personal and precious instrument without reminding you of anatomy class. Topics include breathing and breath support, singing loudly without hurting your voice, singing in tune, the timbre of your voice, articulation, registers and ranges, memorizing lyrics, and more. The main purpose of the chapter on voice care is to prevent problems.

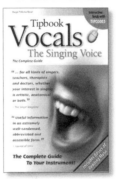

### International editions

The Tipbook Series is also available in Spanish, French, German, Dutch, Italian, and Chinese. For more information, please visit us at www. tipbook.com.

223

# Tipbook Series
# Music and Musical
# Instruments

**Tipbook Acoustic Guitar**
ISBN 978-1-4234-4275-2, HL00332802 — $14.95

**Tipbook Amplifiers and Effects**
ISBN 978-1-4234-6277-4, HL00332776 — $14.99

**Tipbook Cello**
ISBN 978-1-4234-5623-0, HL00331904 — $14.95

**Tipbook Clarinet**
ISBN 978-1-4234-6524-9, HL00332803 — $14.99

**Tipbook Drums**
ISBN 978-90-8767-102-0, HL00331474 — $14.95

**Tipbook Electric Guitar and Bass Guitar**
ISBN 978-1-4234-4274-5, HL00332372 — $14.95

**Tipbook Flute & Piccolo**
ISBN 978-1-4234-6525-6, HL00332804 — $14.99

**Tipbook Home Keyboard and Digital Piano**
ISBN 978-1-4234-4277-6, HL00332375 — $14.99

**Tipbook Music for Kids and Teens**
ISBN 978-1-4234-6526-3, HL00332805 — $14.99

**Tipbook Music on Paper — Basic Theory**
ISBN 978-1-4234-6529-4, HL00332807 — $14.99

**Tipbook Piano**
ISBN 978-1-4234-6278-1, HL00332777 — $14.99

**Tipbook Saxophone**
ISBN 978-90-8767-101-3, HL00331475 — $14.95

**Tipbook Trumpet and Trombone, Flugelhorn and Cornet**
ISBN 978-1-4234-6527-0, HL00332806 — $14.99

**Tipbook Violin and Viola**
ISBN 978-1-4234-4276-9, HL00332374 — $14.95

**Tipbook Vocals — The Singing Voice**
ISBN 978-1-4234-5622-3, HL00331949 — $14.95

**Check www.tipbook.com for additional information!**